WHITE HOUSE KIDS

★ THE PERKS, PLEASURES, PROBLEMS, AND PRATFALLS OF THE PRESIDENTS' CHILDREN ★

JOE RHATIGAN

WITH ILLUSTRATIONS BY JAY SHIN

imagine!
Publishing

For the kids in the Blue House on Rose Hill Road—J.R.

An Imagine Book
Published by Charlesbridge Publishing
85 Main Street, Watertown, MA 02472
(617) 926-0329
www.charlesbridge.com

Text copyright © 2012 by Joseph Rhatigan.
Illustrations copyright © 2012 by Charlesbridge Publishing, Inc.
Illustrations on pages 9, 12, 19, 33, 42, 49, 53, 55, 64, 67, 69, 71, 75, 81, and 83 by Jay Shin.
Cover and interior design by Melissa Gerber.

Printed in China, March 2012.

Library of Congress Cataloging-in-Publication Data is available.

2 4 6 8 10 9 7 5 3 1

ISBN 13: 978-1-936140-80-0

For information about custom editions, special sales,
premium and corporate purchases, please contact
Charlesbridge Publishing at specialsales@charlesbridge.com

CONTENTS

YOUR NEW ADDRESS: 1600 PENNSYLVANIA AVENUE NW, WASHINGTON, DC 20500.........4

CHAPTER 1: THE FIRST WHITE HOUSE KIDS 8

CHAPTER 2: IN THE SPOTLIGHT 15

CHAPTER 3: THE BEST PLAYGROUND AVAILABLE 38

CHAPTER 4: THE PERKS AND PROBLEMS 63

APPENDICES
  A. AND THEN WHAT HAPPENED? 88
  B. THE PRESIDENTS AND FIRST LADIES 92

BIBLIOGRAPHY 94

INDEX 95

PHOTO CREDITS 96

YOUR NEW ADDRESS:
1600 PENNSYLVANIA AVENUE NW, WASHINGTON, DC 20500

Imagine for a moment that your mom or dad gets a new job. It's in a different city and you have to move, even though the job is temporary, only lasting four or eight years. Your new house, which has been chosen by your parents' employers (you have no choice in the matter), is unlike any other home you've ever lived in. For one thing, it's larger—much, much larger. (How many houses do *you* know that have a bowling alley in the basement?) It's also furnished with items that look more at home in a museum than in your living room. Kings and queens may have once slept in your new bedroom, and world-changing documents were signed a few feet from where you will eat your dinner.

Your parents will work from this mansion . . . and so will their employees. While you do your homework upstairs, there will be hundreds of people downstairs working. That's not including the more than six thousand people who come to visit your new house every day. And, oh yeah, there are armed guards at every entrance and a SWAT team on the roof.

You no longer have to wash the dishes, vacuum, or take out the trash; however, you can't just walk out your front door and go for a bike ride. There's a giant kitchen always stocked with your favorite foods, but you may have to eat alone because your parents are at a fancy dinner downstairs that you aren't invited to. You get to travel in your own private jet, but more often than not you'll be stuck at home while your extra-busy parents travel. You'll instantly become one of the most famous kids in the world, but newspapers, websites, and television shows will write and talk about you—and they may not always have nice things to say. You have your own heated outdoor swimming pool, tennis and basketball courts, and movie theater (where you can request any movie—even if it's still in the theaters!), but it may be difficult to make friends and be yourself, especially now that you have your own bodyguards, who will follow you as soon as you step foot outside your new house.

Yes, your mom or dad has just been elected to the office of President of the United States, and your family is about to move to the White House. You're in for the ride of your life.

✳ ✳ ✳

Would you trade the life you're currently living for instant celebrity and incredible adventures? Would you say good-bye to all your friends, your school, and your neighborhood to live in a giant mansion? Fewer than fifty people have been president, but more than two hundred kids have called the White House home. That's a lot of children, grandchildren, nieces, nephews, and cousins who have grown up and lived here before you. They went to school here, wrote about their fears in their diaries here, played, cried, got sick, got married, and in a few cases even died here.

Maybe reading about the kids who have lived in the White House before will help you decide if you'd like this new life. Could you learn to enjoy being a White House kid? What follows are some of the most interesting stories of children who grew up for a part of their lives in the White House. These kids range in age from newborn to nineteen (adult children of presidents are not included here, except for a few mentions), and although your life may never be anything like theirs, you'll probably find that you have a lot in common.

GO TO PAGE 92 TO SEE A LIST OF ALL THE PRESIDENTS AND FIRST LADIES AND THE YEARS THEY SERVED.

WE ALL LIVED THERE!

HOME SWEET HOME. THIS AERIAL VIEW OF THE WHITE HOUSE SHOWS THE NORTH FACE OF THE BUILDING. THE IMAGE ON PAGE 7 SHOWS THE SOUTH FACE.

YES, IT'S THEIR FATHER'S PLANE, BUT MALIA AND SASHA OBAMA GET TO USE IT WHEN THEY TRAVEL WITH HIM!

THE UNITED STATES OF AMERICA

IN GOD WE TRUST

TWENTY DOLLARS

20 20

FORGET WHAT YOUR NEW HOUSE LOOKS LIKE? SIMPLY CHECK OUT THE BACK OF A $20 BILL!

WHAT'S A FIRST LADY?

THE FIRST LADY IS THE PRESIDENT'S WIFE. THE TERM WASN'T COMMONLY USED UNTIL AROUND THE MID-1800S; BEFORE THAT, NOBODY QUITE KNEW WHAT TO CALL THEM! WHEN THE UNITED STATES ELECTS A WOMAN PRESIDENT, HER HUSBAND WILL BE CALLED THE FIRST GENTLEMAN. THE WHOLE FAMILY IS OFTEN CALLED THE FIRST FAMILY, AND THE PRESIDENT'S CHILD CAN BE REFERRED TO AS THE FIRST CHILD OR THE FIRST KID.

MARTHA WASHINGTON, THE *FIRST* FIRST LADY

FIRST FLOOR, FROM LEFT TO RIGHT: DIPLOMATIC RECEPTION ROOM, CHINA ROOM, VERMEIL ROOM, LIBRARY (BEHIND VERMEIL ROOM); SECOND FLOOR, FROM LEFT TO RIGHT: STATE DINING ROOM, RED ROOM, BLUE ROOM, GREEN ROOM, AND EAST ROOM.

WHEN READING THE STORIES IN THIS BOOK, REFER TO THIS DIAGRAM SO YOU CAN SEE WHERE THE ACTION TAKES PLACE.

THE WHITE HOUSE BY THE NUMBERS

Square feet:	55,000
Acres of the property:	18
Doors:	412
Windows:	147
Rooms:	132
Bathrooms:	32
Fireplaces:	28
Staircases:	8
Elevators:	3
Kitchens:	3
Staff needed to run the White House:	more than 100
Gallons of paint needed to paint the outside of the White House:	570

CHAPTER 1:
THE FIRST WHITE HOUSE KIDS

Presidents in the early days tended to be older men, so usually their children were grown up and had lives of their own. That didn't mean kids didn't live in the White House, though. Many presidents brought their grandchildren and adopted kids to the mansion.

First Kids, No Home

Although George Washington chose the design and location for the White House, he and his family never lived in it while he served as the nation's first president. He, his wife, Martha, and two of Martha's grandchildren from a previous marriage lived in the temporary capital, New York City, and then Philadelphia while the White House was being built.

FIRST FAMILY PORTRAIT: THE WASHINGTONS
FROM LEFT TO RIGHT: FIRST LADY MARTHA WASHINGTON, NELLY, PRESIDENT GEORGE WASHINGTON, AND LITTLE WASH

The Washingtons informally adopted Nelly and George Washington "Little Wash" Parke Custis after their father died of a fever during the Revolutionary War. Nelly was ten years old when her grandfather became president, and Little Wash was eight. Nelly often helped entertain guests at the three presidential mansions they lived in during Washington's eight years in service, sometimes singing and playing piano at state dinners. Little Wash, on the other hand, caused his grandparents more trouble, as they worried about his lack of interest in school and learning.

So even if they sometimes visited the White House while it was being built and may have played in the unfinished rooms, Nelly and Little Wash never called it home.

Moving In

President John Adams, one of the young nation's Founding Fathers, spent most of his one term in office in Philadelphia; however, in 1800, the new presidential mansion was considered ready for its president. Adams moved in on November 1, 1800, and his wife, Abigail, and four-year-old granddaughter, Susanna Adams, moved in later that same month. Susanna, the daughter of the Adamses' deceased son, Charles, was known for her tantrums and sullenness. And her mood couldn't have improved much after moving into the cold, drafty, and barely livable mansion. Only six of its twenty rooms were considered finished, and while the first family attempted to make a home for themselves, builders, masons, carpenters, and more hurried to fit doors and windows, plaster walls, place flooring, and finish staircases. There were no lights and very little furniture, the main stairs had not been put up, firewood was expensive and difficult to keep in supply, and to top it all off, they had to use an outhouse whenever they needed to go to the bathroom. In the East Room, where for the next two hundred years presidents and first ladies would entertain kings, queens, senators, and prime ministers, and where lavish weddings, dances, and receptions would be held, Susanna played underfoot while her grandmother hung the laundry.

When Susanna looked out one of the many windows, there was no city. Washington was more like a forest, and Pennsylvania Avenue was nothing but a dirt road that turned into a muddy swamp whenever it rained. So instead of buildings, she would have seen all the construction garbage strewn around the grounds, as well as shacks for the workmen. The population of Washington was eight thousand, and Abigail Adams called the village where she shopped for groceries "the dirtyest hole I ever saw." John Adams was bitter about not being reelected later that year, but the rest of the family was more than happy to move back to Peacefield, the family home in Quincy, Massachusetts.

GEORGE WASHINGTON CONFERS WITH WHITE HOUSE ARCHITECT JAMES HOBAN

FIRST PERSON

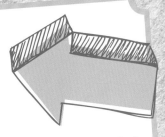

SUSANNA'S GRANDDAUGHTER WAS ONCE ASKED TO RECALL ANY STORIES HER GRANDMOTHER TOLD ABOUT HER SHORT STAY AT THE WHITE HOUSE. THIS WAS HER ANSWER.

MY GRANDMOTHER'S EARLIEST RECOLLECTIONS WERE OF GOING TO WASHINGTON WITH HER GRANDPARENTS AFTER HER FATHER'S DEATH, OF THE LITTLE BLACK FROCK THAT WAS MADE FOR HER THEN, AND OF HAVING THE WHOOPING COUGH AT THE WHITE HOUSE WHERE [DURING A COUGHING FIT] SHE WOULD THROW HERSELF ON THE FLOOR, AND LIE EXHAUSTED, UNTIL PICKED UP BY SOME COMPASSIONATE MEMBER OF THE HOUSEHOLD.

A VIEW OF WASHINGTON, DC, IN 1859, WITH THE U.S. CAPITOL IN THE FOREGROUND

VIEW OF WASHINGTON CITY.

POPULATION EXPLOSION

BY 1850, THE POPULATION OF WASHINGTON, DC, HAD GROWN TO 75,000. FIFTY YEARS LATER: 278,000. BY 1950, IT HAD REACHED A PEAK OF 800,000. TODAY, IT'S AROUND 600,000, AS MANY RESIDENTS HAVE MOVED TO THE SUBURBS SURROUNDING THE CITY.

WASHINGTON, DC, TODAY

THE WHITE HOUSE'S VARIOUS NAMES

THE WHITE HOUSE HAS ONLY BEEN THE OFFICIAL NAME OF THE PRESIDENTS' HOME AND OFFICE SINCE THEODORE "TEDDY" ROOSEVELT'S ADMINISTRATION. BEFORE THEN, IT WAS KNOWN BY A FEW DIFFERENT NAMES.

- THE PALACE: THIS NAME NEVER STUCK BECAUSE IT SOUNDED TOO MUCH LIKE A KING'S CASTLE AND NOT THE HOME OF THE HEAD OF THE REPUBLIC.
- THE PRESIDENT'S HOUSE: THE ADAMS, JEFFERSON, AND MADISON ADMINISTRATIONS USED THIS TERM.
- THE EXECUTIVE HOUSE OR MANSION: USED UNTIL TEDDY ROOSEVELT.
- THE WHITE HOUSE: USED AS A NICKNAME SINCE THE EXTERIOR WAS PAINTED WHITE IN 1798, UNTIL TEDDY ROOSEVELT MADE IT THE OFFICIAL NAME IN 1901.

A Whole Bunch of Firsts

The early first families made history whenever they did something at the White House because they were the first to do it!

✳ ✳ ✳

The first child born in the White House was a boy. His name was James Madison Randolph, and he was born in 1806. He was the son of Thomas Jefferson's daughter Martha Jefferson Randolph.

✳ ✳ ✳

The first child of a president under the age of nineteen to live in the White House was Maria Hester Monroe, daughter of James Monroe. She was fourteen when her father became president in 1817, but she didn't move into the White House until she was fifteen. And just over a year later, she got married! (See below.)

✳ ✳ ✳

The first White House wedding took place in the Blue Room in 1820 during James Monroe's administration. His teenage daughter Maria and one of his secretaries, Samuel Lawrence Gouverneur, fell in love. Even though Gouverneur was the first lady's nephew (making the loving couple first cousins) and Maria was still a young teenager, Monroe consented to the marriage.

✳ ✳ ✳

In 1828, two White House kids were the bride *and* groom. John Quincy Adams's adult son John, Jr., was living in the White House (after being expelled from college for "rioting") when the orphaned children of Mrs. Adams's sister came to live with them. One, a teenager named Mary, fell in love with John (after first falling in love with his other two brothers). They, too, were first cousins and were married in the Blue Room. Later that same year, they had their own White House kid, Mary Louisa, the first girl born in the White House. Grandpa President John Quincy Adams nicknamed her Looly.

IMAGINE LIVING IN THE WHITE HOUSE WHEN . . .
LEWIS AND CLARK EXPLORED THE WEST

IN 1803, THOMAS JEFFERSON SENT MERIWETHER LEWIS AND WILLIAM CLARK ON AN EXPEDITION THROUGH THE NEWLY ACQUIRED LANDS WEST OF THE MISSISSIPPI RIVER ALL THE WAY TO THE PACIFIC OCEAN. LEWIS SENT MANY NEVER-BEFORE-SEEN SOUVENIRS OF THEIR JOURNEY BACK TO THE WHITE HOUSE, INCLUDING GIGANTIC ANTLERS, SNAKE SKINS, ANIMAL PELTS AND SKELETONS, NATIVE AMERICAN COSTUMES AND ARTIFACTS, AND EVEN A BLACK-TAILED PRAIRIE DOG THAT ENDED UP LIVING AT THE WHITE HOUSE. THE ITEMS WERE DISPLAYED IN THE ENTRANCE HALL FOR ALL TO SEE. (BACK THEN, ANYONE COULD OPEN UP THE WHITE HOUSE DOORS AND WALK RIGHT ON IN.) A SECOND EXPEDITION IN 1806 SENT BACK ALIVE TWO GRIZZLY BEAR CUBS, WHICH JEFFERSON ALLOWED TO BE KEPT AT THE WHITE HOUSE FOR A COUPLE OF MONTHS.

"The White House . . . was the model American home—love, kindness, and charity guarding it like sentries. Known to the world as the man whose iron will and fierce, ungovernable temper defied opposition and courted antagonism, he was the gentlest, tenderest, most patient of men at his own fireside."

—Mary Donelson, niece of Andrew Jackson

Old Hickory's Full House

Andrew Jackson was a tough, mean, and often violent man who fought in the Revolutionary War when he was only twelve. He was a hero during the War of 1812, dealt harshly with Native Americans, and took part in several duels with enemies—all of which he won, even though one of them left him with a bullet lodged in his chest. In other words, he wasn't called "tough as old hickory" (Old Hickory, for short) for nothing. But don't tell that to the several kids who came to live with him in the White House. Their nickname for him might have been Old Cuddly Bear!

Although childless and a widower (his wife died shortly before he took office in 1829), by 1835, Jackson's White House was overflowing with kids. At least six children under the age of ten lived in the mansion. Four of the kids, Jackson (nine), Mary (six), John (three), and Rachel (eighteen months), belonged to his wife's niece Emily Donelson, who served as Jackson's official hostess. Her husband, a nephew of Jackson's, was his secretary. (Three of the kids were born in the White House.) The other two children were Rachel (three) and Andrew Jackson III (eighteen months), and they belonged to Jackson's adopted son, Andrew Jackson, Jr. And there in the midst of all of them was the tough-as-nails president, babysitting, soothing crying babies, horsing around on the floor, helping with homework, and more.

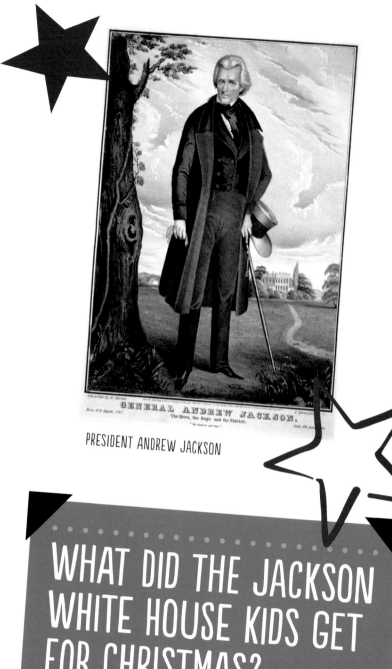

GENERAL ANDREW JACKSON.
The Hero, the Sage and the Patriot.

PRESIDENT ANDREW JACKSON

WHAT DID THE JACKSON WHITE HOUSE KIDS GET FOR CHRISTMAS?

JACKSON RECEIVED A SMALL GUN AND A SADDLE AND BRIDLE. MARY AND HER COUSIN RACHEL RECEIVED DOLLS AND TEA SETS. JOHN, A HOBBY HORSE AND DRUM. THE BABIES, TOY RATTLES. IN THEIR STOCKINGS THEY FOUND A QUARTER, FRUIT, CANDY, CAKES, AND NUTS. MARY ALSO RECEIVED A MINIATURE COOKING STOVE FROM HER GODFATHER, THE VICE PRESIDENT.

"Living in the White House is a unique experience—a fantastic compound of excitement and tension and terror and pride and humility. Above all it is a historic experience."
—Margaret Truman

Some Good Advice

When Vice President John Tyler became president after the untimely death of President William Henry Harrison, he gathered his seven children (an eighth died soon after birth) and supposedly gave them these words of advice: "Now my children, during the next few years, I hope that you will conduct yourselves with more than usual propriety and decorum . . . You are to know no favourites . . . You are to accept no gifts whatsoever . . . You are to allow no one to approach you on the subject of office or favors." And the kids must have listened to him, since they kept a rather low profile. Four of the seven kids came to live at the White House: Letitia (twenty), Elizabeth (eighteen), Alice (fourteen), and Tazewell (eleven). Alice and Tazewell did get to meet Charles Dickens, their favorite author; however, surely they refused any gifts he may have offered them.

"My children are my principal treasures."

—John Tyler

DID YOU KNOW?

JOHN TYLER'S WIFE, LETITIA, DIED IN THE WHITE HOUSE IN 1842. TWO YEARS LATER, TYLER MARRIED A WOMAN THIRTY YEARS YOUNGER THAN HE WAS (AND SIX YEARS YOUNGER THAN TYLER'S OLDEST DAUGHTER). AND AFTER HIS TWO TERMS IN OFFICE, HE HAD ANOTHER SEVEN CHILDREN. FIFTEEN KIDS? THAT'S A RECORD FOR AN AMERICAN PRESIDENT.

CHAPTER 2:
IN THE SPOTLIGHT

Americans have always been fascinated with their first families. A newspaper article way back in the late 1790s reported that First Lady Martha Washington accidentally ate a dollop of cream that had gone bad. Another mentioned that Nelly and Little Wash went to the circus!

Nobody needs to tell you that growing up isn't always easy. Sure, it's fun, but then there are the chores, your parents' expectations, school, cliques, and more. It's an important time in everyone's life, when you're learning new things nearly every day, making mistakes, and feeling awkward as your body changes. Well, imagine trying to handle all of that while millions of people consider you public property and watch and report on your every move!

White House kids and their parents have handled instant celebrity in different ways. Modern first families usually make a deal with reporters: Take all the pictures you want of the adults and say what you will, but **leave the kids alone**! And that worked pretty well for younger children such as Chelsea Clinton and Malia and Sasha Obama. But since George W. Bush's twins, Barbara and Jenna, were teenagers when their dad became president, they were considered fair game, and they were often followed by paparazzi. How would you handle your new celebrity status as a White House kid?

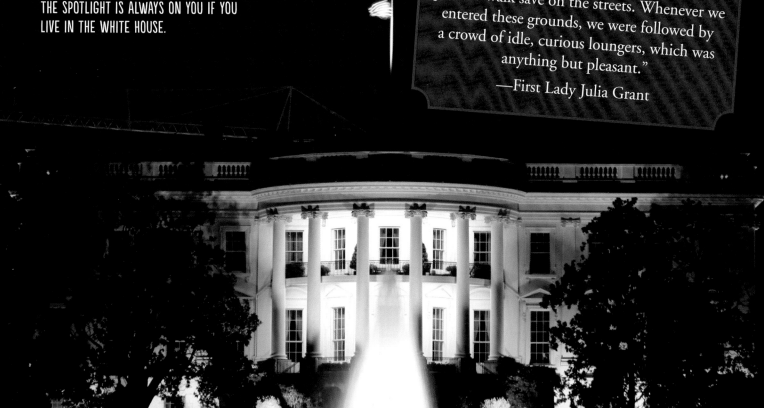

THE SPOTLIGHT IS ALWAYS ON YOU IF YOU LIVE IN THE WHITE HOUSE.

"I was somewhat annoyed that the grounds back of the mansion were open to the public. Nellie and Jess had no place to play, and I no place to walk save on the streets. Whenever we entered these grounds, we were followed by a crowd of idle, curious loungers, which was anything but pleasant."

—First Lady Julia Grant

IMAGINE LIVING IN THE WHITE HOUSE WHEN . . . IT WAS OPEN TO THE PUBLIC

UP UNTIL THE LATE 1800S, IT WAS A TRADITION TO KEEP THE GATES AROUND THE WHITE HOUSE OPEN TO THE AMERICAN PUBLIC. IT WAS ONE WAY TO PROVE THAT THE WHITE HOUSE BELONGED TO THE PEOPLE. NEVER MIND THAT ANYONE STROLLING DOWN PENNSYLVANIA AVENUE COULD WALK RIGHT UP TO THE HOUSE AND PEEK IN THE WINDOWS, WHICH IS EXACTLY WHAT HAPPENED ON MANY OCCASIONS. ALSO, JUST ABOUT ANYONE COULD OPEN THE DOOR AND WALK RIGHT ON IN WITHOUT AN INVITATION. THEY COULD JOIN THE LONG LINE OF PEOPLE WAITING TO SEE THE PRESIDENT WITH PETITIONS OR REQUESTS FOR JOBS, OR THEY COULD TAKE A TOUR OF THE PLACE. IF THE UNGUIDED TOURISTS WERE LUCKY, THEY COULD GET UPSTAIRS, AND EVEN OPEN UP YOUR BEDROOM DOOR!

THIS PHOTOGRAPH FROM 1889 SHOWS A VENDOR SELLING WAFFLES ON THE WHITE HOUSE GROUNDS.

FIRST FAMILY PORTRAIT: THE LINCOLNS FROM LEFT TO RIGHT: ROBERT, WILLIAM, PRESIDENT ABRAHAM LINCOLN, FIRST LADY MARY TODD LINCOLN, AND TAD (THOMAS)

Show Us the Children!

When Abraham Lincoln was elected president, newspapers loved the fact that they'd be able to write stories about the two little boys who would be living in the White House—the first young children of a president in nearly twenty years. Willie was ten years old and Tad was eight when they moved to the White House. The two boys would give reporters some great stories over the years, even if they didn't always wish to cooperate.

When the boys traveled by train with their mother, Mary Todd, to the White House for the first time, reporters crowded outside their car at a station stop. "Where are the children? Show us the children!" the reporters shouted. Mary brought her oldest son, Robert (seventeen), to the car window. After cheering for him, they asked, "Have you any more on board?" Mary said, "Yes, here's another." She then tried to get Tad to come to the window, but he would have none of it. He lay on the floor and refused to budge—laughing the whole time. Mary had to tell the people Tad wouldn't come to the window. At other stops, Tad would run into the crowd on the platform and ask complete strangers, "Do you want to see Old Abe?" After the people nodded yes, Tad would point out somebody else and then run off laughing.

While playing outside the White House one day, Willie prevented Tad from punching a boy who had called them mudsills (people of low character or social standing). When Tad asked why he kept him from defending their honor, Willie responded that they didn't want the incident to get in the newspapers. Willie not only took care of his brother, but also saw at an early age how the wrong kind of publicity could hurt his father.

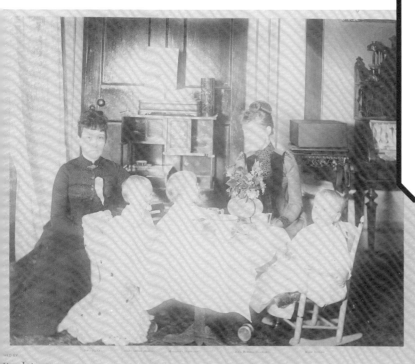

THE BABES OF THE WHITE HOUSE.
Copyrighted 1889, by W. J. Merrill.

FIRST FAMILY PORTRAIT: THE HARRISON GRANDCHILDREN
FROM LEFT TO RIGHT: MARY HARRISON MCKEE, MARY LODGE, MARTHENA,
MRS. RUSSELL HARRISON, AND BABY MCKEE (BENJAMIN)

FIRST PERSON

A WASHINGTON REPORTER WROTE A LONG ARTICLE ABOUT BENJAMIN HARRISON'S LITTLE GRANDSON (ALSO NAMED BENJAMIN), WHO LIVED AT THE WHITE HOUSE WITH HIS MOTHER AND SISTER, AND WHOM THE PRESIDENT LIKED TO CALL BABY MCKEE. HE WAS JUST AS WELL KNOWN AND POPULAR AS THE PRESIDENT, WHO ALLOWED MANY PHOTOS OF THE BOY TO BE PUBLISHED IN NEWSPAPERS. BABY MCKEE WAS PHOTOGRAPHED RIDING WITH HIS GOAT, PLAYING WITH HIS DOG, WEARING CUTE HATS, LEADING A BAND, AND MORE.

THIS PRETTY LITTLE FELLOW AND HIS PLACE IN THE AFFECTIONS OF THE PRESIDENT HAVE BEEN SO MUCH COMMENTED UPON IN THE PRESS THAT WORD HAS GONE OUT TO LET UP LEST THE PEOPLE OF THIS COUNTRY SHOULD COME TO BELIEVE THE TALES ABOUT THIS CHILD'S HAVING MORE INFLUENCE THAN MEMBERS OF THE CABINET.

TOYS HAVE BEEN POURING INTO THE WHITE HOUSE FOR BABY MCKEE AND HIS BABY SISTER, MARY LODGE. HIS PONY CART AND HIS FAVORITE FRENCH MECHANICAL DOG HAVE LATELY BEEN PUT ASIDE FOR A MINIATURE TENNIS SET WITH WHICH HE PLAYS . . . OFTEN WITH HIS GRANDFATHER AS A FASCINATED WATCHER.

MANY A VISITOR IN THE PRESIDENT'S STUDY HAS FELT A WARM LITTLE ARM ABOUT HIS LEG IN THE MIDST OF HIS INTERVIEW.

"He is a jolly boy, not a bit spoiled, and he and I had some famous times."

—Benjamin Harrison on Baby McKee

Baby Ruth

The press and public have always been fascinated with White House kids. However, up until the early twentieth century, they were allowed in most cases to lead normal lives. These lucky kids could walk to school, have friends over, and play outside on the White House lawn with hardly anyone noticing. But then something funny happened when Ruth Cleveland was born. Ruth, the first daughter of President Grover Cleveland, was born in 1891 between her father's two terms in office. (Cleveland wasn't reelected after his first term ended, but ran again successfully four years later.) Ruth's birth caused a national sensation, and the Clevelands' growing family became celebrities.

Visitors began crowding through the White House gates and rushing to where Baby Ruth sat and played outside just to get a glimpse of her. But then a glimpse wasn't enough. One day a tourist pulled Ruth from her nurse's arms and began passing her around and pinching her cheeks. The Clevelands knew they had to make a change. First, they rented a home nearby where the family could live peacefully, and then they removed Ruth from public view. That only fueled rumors from the angry people who could no longer read about and touch Baby Ruth. They said that she was crippled, feebleminded, had a withered hand or malformed ears, and was a deaf mute.

FIRST FAMILY PORTRAIT: THE CLEVELANDS
FROM LEFT TO RIGHT: PRESIDENT GROVER CLEVELAND,
RUTH, AND FIRST LADY FRANCES CLEVELAND

There was also a plot to kidnap Ruth. Letters were found that outlined a plan to "carry off little Ruth Cleveland and hold her until a ransom was forthcoming." Baby Ruth's life in the limelight was over, whether the American people liked it or not.

Ruth's baby sister, Esther, was the first and only child of a president born in the White House. Esther was born in 1903, and she received thousands of knitted booties as gifts from people all over the nation.

FIRST LADY FRANCES CLEVELAND—NEARLY YOUNG ENOUGH TO BE A WHITE HOUSE KID!

DID YOU KNOW?

GROVER CLEVELAND WAS A BACHELOR WHEN HE FIRST BECAME PRESIDENT, BUT HE MARRIED FRANCES FOLSOM (WHOM HE MET SOON AFTER SHE WAS BORN!) IN THE BLUE ROOM OF THE WHITE HOUSE IN 1886. HE WAS THE ONLY PRESIDENT EVER MARRIED AT THE WHITE HOUSE. FRANCES WAS TWENTY-SEVEN YEARS YOUNGER THAN THE PRESIDENT, AND AT TWENTY-ONE, SHE ALMOST MADE THE CUT AS A WHITE HOUSE KID!

WHAT'S A CHIEF USHER?

THE CHIEF USHER IS THE HEAD OF THE HOUSEHOLD AND OPERATIONS AT THE WHITE HOUSE. IT'S HIS OR HER JOB TO ORGANIZE ALL THE WHITE HOUSE SOCIAL EVENTS, MAINTAIN THE MANSION, SUPERVISE THE STAFF, AND TAKE CARE OF FAMILY NEEDS.

FIRST PERSON

IRWIN "IKE" HOOD HOOVER WORKED AT THE WHITE HOUSE FOR MORE THAN FORTY YEARS (1891–1933) AND WATCHED TEN FIRST FAMILIES COME AND GO. HE BEGAN AS AN ELECTRICIAN AND WAS CHIEF USHER FOR NEARLY TWENTY-FIVE YEARS. THIS OBSERVATION ABOUT THE CLEVELAND CHILDREN IS FROM HIS MEMOIR.

THE CHILDREN WERE THE OBJECTS OF INSANE CURIOSITY. ONCE A VISITOR WAS SNIPPING A CURL FROM RUTH'S HEAD WHEN STOPPED. THE NURSES WERE AT THEIR WITS' ENDS TO PROTECT THEIR CHARGES. LOOKING OUT ONE DAY, MRS. CLEVELAND SAW A NURSE IN TEARS AND ONE BABY BEING HANDED ABOUT AND PAWED BY A CROWD OF FIFTY VISITORS. THE MOTHER WAS FORCED TO ISSUE AN ORDER CLOSING THE GATES TO THE SOUTH GROUNDS WHERE THE CHILDREN TOOK THE AIR.

Princess Alice

When Teddy Roosevelt assumed the presidency after the assassination of William McKinley in 1901, he brought all six of his children to the White House. The oldest, Alice, seventeen at the time, was a lot like her attention-grabbing father. She once described him as wanting to be "the corpse at every funeral, the bride at every wedding, and the baby at every christening." She could have just as easily been talking about herself, because she absolutely thrived on all the attention she received, and she became an instant celebrity upon entering the White House. If reading in newspapers and magazines about the antics of the Roosevelt family became a national pastime, gossiping about what the beautiful, self-confident, intelligent, and wild Alice was up to became an obsession.

In an age where young women were supposed to be proper and dainty, Alice sped around in cars with her girlfriends (up to thirty miles per hour!), slid down banisters to greet diplomats, rode horses like a man (not sidesaddle, which was what was considered proper for women riders), went to every party in and around Washington and danced until morning, went to receptions with a snake (named Emily Spinach) coiled around her arm, smoked cigarettes in public, gambled, and more.

Instead of disliking her for all her rule-breaking, people named their babies after her, wrote songs about her, and even named Alice's favorite color after her: Alice Blue. If Alice wore a certain type of hat, it became all the rage. She

ALICE WAS BIG NEWS.

ALICE IN HER "DON'T MESS WITH ME" POSE

ALICE IN JAPAN

ALL SET FOR SOME HORSE RIDING—
THE WAY ALICE WANTS!

awarded medals at the 1904 Olympics, christened ships of foreign royalty, and was mobbed at the St. Louis World's Fair. At a reception, someone remarked, "You must be tired to death, shaking hands with so many people." Alice replied, "Tired? Why, I could throw my arms around their necks and kiss them!"

A friend of Teddy's complained to him after the third time Alice interrupted their meeting at the White House. "Theodore, isn't there anything you can do to control Alice?" Teddy responded, "I can either run the country or attend to Alice, but I cannot possibly do both."

One way Teddy attempted to tame Alice was to send her on a diplomatic mission to Japan, Hawaii, China, the Philippines, and Korea. She traveled with twenty-three congressmen, the secretary of war, seven senators, and other diplomats; however, she was the center of every meeting and the star at every reception and party. She jumped into a cruise ship's swimming pool fully clothed, was heralded by

trumpeters in Korea, and politely declined to join a South Pacific king's harem as his seventh wife. She returned with a new nickname (Princess Alice), enough gifts that the press called her "Alice in Plunder Land," and a fiancé, congressman Nicholas Longworth.

Alice and Nicholas were married on February 17, 1906, and true to fashion, Alice cut the wedding cake with a sword, which became a White House wedding tradition. She remained the life of the party in Washington, DC, for the next sixty-five years.

ALICE IN HER WEDDING GOWN

Peachy

John Coolidge was sixteen years old when his father, Calvin Coolidge, became president in 1923 after the death of President Warren Harding. John and his younger brother, Cal, Jr., spent that first summer at the White House and then went off to boarding school, although they spent many weekends at the mansion. When John was old enough and went off to college, everything he did was noticed. Fellow students remarked about his secondhand coat and the fact that he wasn't a very good saxophone player or boxer. They also took a deep interest in whom he was dating. In a yearbook caption, John was made fun of for receiving "seven thousand scented letters from admiring schoolgirls." Newspaper reporters began snooping at the school (and the nearby girls' schools) and wrote articles about John's college life. One such article was titled "John Coolidge a Peach."

One of John's female fans at a nearby college was quoted as saying, "John is a perfect peach. He is so polished and smooth and he dances divinely. They talk about his being shy and reserved—well, he certainly is a peach."

WHAT IS A PEACH?

CALVIN COOLIDGE WAS PRESIDENT AT THE HEIGHT OF THE ROARING TWENTIES, WHICH WAS A DECADE OF GREAT GROWTH AND PROSPERITY IN THE UNITED STATES. IT WAS ALSO THE AGE OF THE FLAPPERS, WHO WERE YOUNG WOMEN WHO WORE SHORT SKIRTS, LOVED PARTIES, AND CHALLENGED WHAT WAS CONSIDERED ACCEPTABLE BEHAVIOR. THE TERM *PEACH* WAS SLANG FOR *MIGHTY FINE, NICE, PRETTY AMAZING*. HERE'S SOME OTHER SLANG FROM THE ROARING TWENTIES.

THE BEE'S KNEES: **THE BEST**
HARD-BOILED: **TOUGH**
SPIFFY: **ELEGANT IN APPEARANCE**
HORSEFEATHERS: **THAT'S NONSENSE**
A PILL: **AN UNLIKABLE PERSON**
PUTTING ON THE RITZ: **DOING SOMETHING IN A GRAND MANNER**
THE REAL MCCOY: **SOMETHING THAT'S GENUINE**
DOLLED UP: **DRESSED UP**
THE CAT'S MEOW (OR THE CAT'S PAJAMAS): **SOMETHING STYLISH OR WONDERFUL**
STUCK ON: **HAVING A CRUSH ON SOMEONE**

FIRST FAMILY PORTRAIT: THE COOLIDGES
FRONT: PRESIDENT CALVIN COOLIDGE AND FIRST LADY GRACE COOLIDGE; BACK: CAL, JR., AND JOHN

LOUISE BROOKS, AN ACTRESS IN THE 1920S, POPULARIZED THE FLAPPER LOOK.

Buzzie's Burden

Curtis Roosevelt was born in 1930 into a large, wealthy, and powerful family. In fact, by the time Curtis was three years old, his grandfather Franklin Delano Roosevelt (FDR) was the thirty-second president of the United States. Curtis and his sister and mother moved into the White House shortly after FDR's inauguration because his parents were getting a divorce. (Curtis would live at the White House until he was seven, and then move back in again when he was a young teenager.) FDR was the only president elected to more than two terms and served for twelve years, until his death in 1945. He created the New Deal to help the United States climb out of the Great Depression and led the Allies against Germany and Japan in World War II. Curtis's grandmother was also a commanding figure. Eleanor Roosevelt worked tirelessly for civil rights and equal rights for women, helped form the United Nations, and fought against poverty.

So who was Curtis? The press quickly nicknamed him

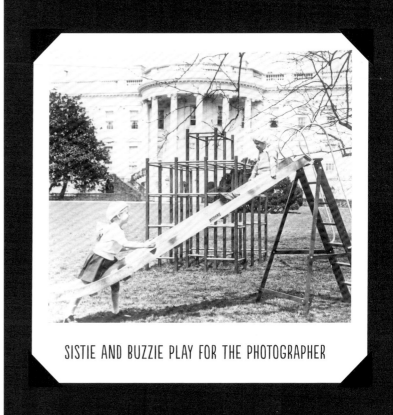

SISTIE AND BUZZIE PLAY FOR THE PHOTOGRAPHER

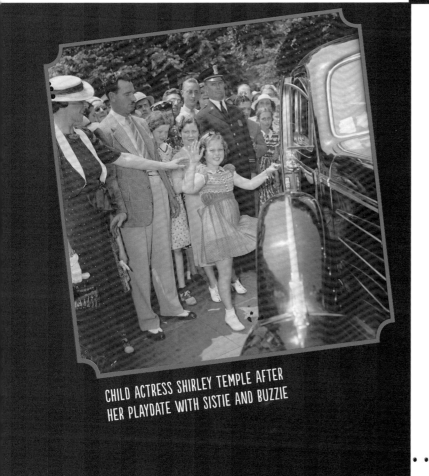

CHILD ACTRESS SHIRLEY TEMPLE AFTER HER PLAYDATE WITH SISTIE AND BUZZIE

Buzzie, while his sister, Anna Eleanor, became Sistie. By all accounts, Buzzie was a cheerful, rambunctious kid who ate up all the attention he received. Life at the White House, however, also dictated that he and his sister be well-behaved, well-groomed, quiet, and humble. So even though his grandmother arranged for photos of the children playing at the White House to appear in newspapers (as a form of entertainment for the people suffering during the Great Depression), Buzzie wasn't supposed to enjoy it. Crowds of people would stand outside the White House gates and yell, "Buzzie! Sistie!" while the kids played on the South Lawn. Photos appeared in newspapers all the time with cute headlines detailing the children's activities. The kids also had the opportunity to spend a day at the White House with the only other child as famous as they were: movie star Shirley Temple.

Unfortunately, being the grandson of the most famous two people in the world was also a burden. As he grew older, Curtis realized he didn't have to make his own way in the world. He could coast by on his famous last name and expect things to be handed to him. It was easy to get jobs, earn money, and find friends. But being a celebrity didn't make it easy *keeping* all of that. "Being able to work was quite beyond me," Curtis said in an interview. "Everything had always been too easy. Given to me . . . I consistently made a mess of whatever I was engaged in."

The other problem Curtis had with being a child celebrity was that everyone he met felt like they already knew him—even if they had never met him before. "Look, it's Buzzie!" they would say. "It's bad enough to be compared at school with a brighter or more able sibling. Imagine that— then multiply it by ten thousand and you might begin to get some idea of what it's like," Curtis said. It's difficult forming relationships if others think they already know you. It's a common problem with child stars of all kinds, and it took Curtis most of his adult life to find out who he truly was, once he was out of the spotlight.

"I grew up knowing nothing other than public adulation. It's not something I would recommend . . . I was constantly being offered things which I had not earned and did not deserve."
—Curtis Roosevelt

SISTIE, JOHNNY, AND BUZZIE SIT WITH THEIR GRANDMOTHER, FIRST LADY ELEANOR ROOSEVELT

The Greatest Vote-Getter of All

John and Jackie Kennedy brought youth and vigor to the somewhat stuffy White House. They also arrived with a three-year-old daughter, Caroline, and a two-month-old son, John-John. This first family captured the nation's attention unlike any that had come before, and they were treated more like movie stars than politicians.

Caroline was a friendly child who liked talking and having her picture taken. A reporter once asked her where her father was. She replied, "He's upstairs with his shoes and socks off doing nothing." One evening, to the delight of everyone, she wandered into a press conference in her nightgown, wearing a pair of her mother's high-heeled shoes. No wonder a newspaper editor once supposedly said, "Never mind that stuff about Laos [a country in Southeast Asia]. What did Caroline say today?" John-John also received a lot of attention; however, as he grew older, he was sometimes known to kick or punch reporters and photographers. (His privacy-loving mother probably cheered him on!)

Jackie tried to control the amount of public exposure the children received. At one time, she demanded that only one story about the children be released to the press per month. She wanted the kids to have as normal a life as possible, and that meant as little press as possible. However, as soon as Jackie left the White House on a trip, the president would let the reporters in. He liked showing off his kids and believed it helped him remain popular with the public. Kennedy once told the children's nanny, "Caroline is a great hit with everyone. I think she could be the greatest vote-getter of all!"

CAROLINE AND HER DAD, PRESIDENT JOHN F. KENNEDY

Kennedy wasn't the first president to use a child to gain popularity. In 1892, Benjamin Harrison was up for reelection, but found himself behind because of Grover Cleveland (who had lost to Harrison in 1889) and his newborn daughter, Baby Ruth. But Harrison had his own famous baby, his grandson Baby McKee. Both babies hit the campaign trail, and in the end, Baby Ruth won the contest and her father made it back to the White House!

BABY RUTH AND BABY MCKEE, THE MUSICAL

GEORGE COOPER AND ADAM GEIBEL PRESENTED A SONG ABOUT THE BABY WARS OF 1892 AT THE NEW YORK STATE FAIR CALLED "BABY RUTH AND BABY MCKEE." HERE IS A SAMPLING OF THE LYRICS:

WE'RE BABY RUTH AND BABY MCKEE,
LIVELY SPECIMENS, YOU'LL AGREE
JUST AS HAPPY AS HAPPY CAN BE.
WE'LL RUN THE NATION'S PRESIDENCY!
WHICH OF US WINS YOU'LL VERY SOON SEE,
BABY RUTH AND BABY MCKEE.

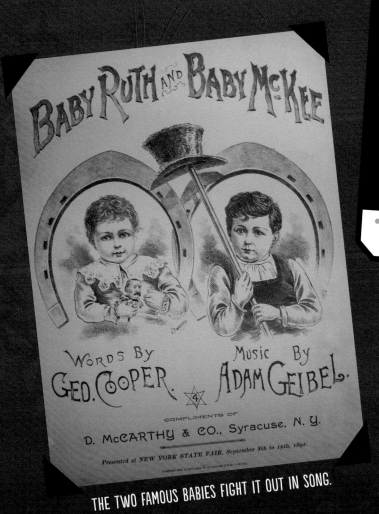

THE TWO FAMOUS BABIES FIGHT IT OUT IN SONG.

"Everyone who lives in the White House to some degree feels like they are living in a goldfish bowl."
—Luci Johnson

Watusi Luci

Lyndon and Lady Bird Johnson brought two daughters with them to the White House when Lyndon had to assume the office after the assassination of John F. Kennedy in 1963. Lynda was nineteen and Luci was seventeen. Though both had to deal with celebrity, Luci was much more vocal about it. Shortly after moving to the White House, Luci exclaimed, "I have been robbed of my youth, my private life!" She complained about having Secret Service men at her side at all times, and at first she felt like being a White House kid was

Lynda found the pressure too much and left her college dorm to live at the White House. (She brought her college roommate with her!) Luci, however, used her fame—not for personal gain, but to talk about issues that were important to her. She said, "I came to see [my time at the White House] as the golden opportunity to be an eyewitness to the major events of my youth, to meet the movers and shakers of my time. I began to realize this extraordinary gift of opportunity and told myself, 'Don't blow it!'"

LUCI AND LYNDA JOHNSON

limiting her life. "I saw it as a source of irritation. I felt like I was living in a . . . museum, a public fishbowl, and a prison." The press constantly asked her whom she was dating, and they came up with nicknames for her, such as Watusi Luci (after she admitted she liked dancing). The sisters' hairstyles, clothing, and makeup were commented on and criticized. Lynda recalled this advice from her mother: "Don't do anything you wouldn't mind seeing on the front page of the newspaper."

So when Luci danced the Watusi, she did so with actor Steve McQueen at a celebrity barbecue fund-raiser for her father's reelection campaign. When she agreed to a magazine interview after school, she insisted on talking about racial equality, poverty, and getting young people involved in solving the world's problems. She also gave campaign speeches for her father and attended receptions as the president's representative. In a short time, Luci had graduated from a whining teenager to a role model.

WANNA DO THE WATUSI?

THIS DANCE FROM THE 1960S IS FAIRLY EASY. FIRST, TURN ON SOME MUSIC—PREFERABLY SOME SURF MUSIC. NEXT, STAND WITH YOUR LEGS APART AND BEND YOUR KNEES SLIGHTLY. SHIFT YOUR WEIGHT TO YOUR RIGHT LEG AND JUT OUT YOUR RIGHT HIP. AT THE SAME TIME, HOLD YOUR HANDS AS THOUGH YOU WERE HOLDING A GOLF CLUB AND SWING THEM RIGHT. RETURN YOUR WEIGHT TO BOTH LEGS AND BRING YOUR HANDS DOWN TO YOUR WAIST. THEN SHIFT YOUR WEIGHT TO YOUR LEFT LEG AND MOVE YOUR LEFT HIP OUT WHILE SWINGING YOUR HANDS TO THE LEFT. REPEAT.

"We have many problems in the United States, and among them one of the most important and urgent is that of genuine racial integration . . . I believe that now more than ever our youth must take an active part and do things in this world where laws have been established without our participation."

—Luci Johnson in an interview with *Ebony* magazine

"I have no illusions. I know that people are not applauding me—they're applauding the president's daughter."

—Lynda Johnson

"When my grades weren't so good, complete strangers scolded me. And when they got better and we sort of leaked the news about my B average, people said I was bragging."

—Luci Johnson

LUCI DANCING WITH ACTOR STEVE MCQUEEN

FIRST FAMILY PORTRAIT: THE OBAMAS
FROM LEFT TO RIGHT: PRESIDENT BARACK OBAMA, SASHA, FIRST LADY MICHELLE OBAMA, AND MALIA

DID YOU KNOW?

AS FAR AS ANYONE KNOWS (OR IS WILLING TO ADMIT), THERE ARE NO SECRET PASSAGEWAYS IN THE WHITE HOUSE. THERE ARE RUMORS OF AN UNDERGROUND TUNNEL THAT CONNECTS THE WHITE HOUSE TO THE TREASURY BUILDING NEXT DOOR, AS WELL AS TALK OF A VAST NETWORK OF UNDERGROUND PASSAGEWAYS CONNECTING MANY OF THE MAJOR BUILDINGS IN DC, BUT NONE OF IT HAS BEEN PROVEN. THERE ARE LOTS OF HIDDEN DOORS, THOUGH, THAT OPEN UP TO CLOSETS AND STAIRWAYS!

Faces in Strange Places

It's pretty crazy seeing your picture in the newspaper, especially when you're just a kid. But that's not the only place where you might find your face if you're a White House kid.

✴ ✴ ✴

As early as President Lincoln's term, people collected cheap photographic cards, like baseball cards, of the first family. You could mail them to friends or collect them.

✴ ✴ ✴

These days, if you're part of the first family, you are bound to star in a presidential paper doll book. Fans of the Clintons can cut out figures of Bill, First Lady Hillary, and First Daughter Chelsea and dress them in suits, gowns, and more. You can also purchase paper doll books of the Bushes (George W.), the Obamas, and other presidential families.

✴ ✴ ✴

When John F. Kennedy became president in 1961, parents could celebrate by purchasing a brand-new doll for their little girls. It was a thirteen-inch baby doll with eyes that opened and closed. It was called the Caroline Kennedy doll, fashioned in the likeness of Kennedy's three-year-old daughter.

✳ ✳ ✳

When the company that makes Beanie Babies tried to do the same thing with Barack Obama's kids, Malia and Sasha, First Lady Michelle Obama complained angrily. She issued this statement as soon as she heard about the new dolls called Sweet Sasha and Marvelous Malia: "We feel it is inappropriate to use young, private citizens for marketing purposes." The toy company denies modeling the toys after the first kids, but they eventually decided not to sell them.

✳ ✳ ✳

Even with the Obamas declaring their kids off-limits, some have sought to make money off them anyway. In 2011, a book titled *The Adventures of Sasha and Malia at the White House* was published. In this fictional story, the two girls discover a moving bookcase in the White House that leads them into a passageway that takes them back to the time

of slavery. The girls have to free the slaves and "change the course of history."

Leave Me Alone!

Sometimes the stress of being in the spotlight can be too much—especially if you're a shy, self-conscious kid. Imagine reading about what you wanted for your birthday in the newspaper. Or having hordes of reporters and photographers follow you around and snap photos of you on your very first day in a brand-new school. How about being pointed at and whispered about in class? Interrupted by the press while trying to learn to ski during a vacation? Or being scolded in news reports for reading at the dinner table during a reception? What about being called spoiled and a brat by the very adults who should be protecting you? All this and more happened to Amy Carter.

Unlike most White House kids, Amy Carter, daughter of Jimmy Carter, didn't want to move to the mansion at all. She was happy where she was, with family and friends in Plains, Georgia. However, she *did* move and was instantly thrust into the limelight, where her parents, although aware that Amy wanted a normal life, sometimes used her to make political points.

Amy was the fourth and youngest child of Jimmy and Rosalynn Carter. Their three boys were adults, but Amy was only nine when Jimmy became president. One of the most important decisions a first family has to make when entering the White House is where their young children will go to school. Will they go to public school to show support for the schools that are funded by taxpayers' money, or will they go to private school? Although private schools can handle security better and keep the press away, the Carters made a political decision to send Amy to public school. On her first day, hundreds of photographers lined up behind a rope barrier and took pictures of a lonely-looking Amy carrying her brand-new Snoopy schoolbag and

INAUGURATION DAY 1977. SMILE FOR THE CAMERA, AMY!

walking into the building with her head down. It didn't get any better when, later in the day, her teacher kept her inside at recess to "protect" her. This left Amy in tears.

The whispers amongst White House staff and Secret Service agents were that Amy was a brat, spoiled by her parents and older brothers. The stewards of Air Force One complained that she played loud rock music and purposely crushed crackers into the carpet for the staff to clean up. "Her greatest thrill was coloring with crayon on the walls of the airplane," said one staff member. And although the Carters denied any of this happened, it couldn't have helped Amy feel any better about her life at the White House.

Finally, while attending a dinner for the president of Mexico, the foreign minister of Mexico was not only insulted to be seated next to Amy, but also took offense that she read a book during the long meal instead of talking to him. Her father simply said, "We always read at the table when we were growing up." At that point, Amy withdrew from public life. She didn't appear at dinners or receptions and sought privacy whenever possible. One of her favorite hiding places was the tree house she and her father designed and White House carpenters built. When asked by a reporter if she had a message for the children of America, she thought about it for a moment, then answered, "No." Amy Carter has stayed out of the spotlight ever since. She makes no public appearances and doesn't grant interviews. Can you blame her?

"Those people aren't there to see me. They just think I'm cute. So I just wave and smile, and then I'm out of there."

—Malia Obama on how she handles the crowds at rallies and speeches

AMY CATCHES A RIDE TO CAMP DAVID, THE PRESIDENTIAL VACATION HOME, FOR A BREAK

Be Careful What You Wear!

For White House kids, the public will notice just about anything. Whereas Alice Roosevelt became a fashion icon, Susan Ford, the teenage daughter of President Gerald Ford, was criticized for wearing jeans in the White House. Charlie Taft, the eleven-year-old son of President William Taft, was working the White House switchboard (something he loved to do and was good at) one day when he took a call from a reporter wondering if Charlie was going to start wearing long pants soon. "Certainly not! There's nothing to it at all! Somebody has been giving you misinformation!" Charlie yelled before slamming down the phone. (Of course, when he finally *did* graduate to long pants, it made the front page of the *New York Times*.) Meanwhile, the J.Crew coats Malia and Sasha Obama wore to their father's inauguration became famous. So many people visited the company's website looking for the coats that the site crashed. "People have been clamoring to get these actual items," a company representative said.

DID YOU KNOW?

IN THE NINETEENTH AND EARLY TWENTIETH CENTURIES, BOYS WORE SHORT PANTS IN THE SUMMER AND KNICKERBOCKERS (PANTS THAT WENT TO THE KNEES) IN THE WINTER. ONCE THEY REACHED THEIR EARLY TEENS, THEY GRADUATED TO LONG PANTS. IT WAS A RITE OF PASSAGE SOME BOYS LOOKED FORWARD TO. OTHERS, LIKE CHARLIE TAFT, WEREN'T MUCH INTERESTED IN LONG PANTS!

"I'll never throw away my blue jeans."

—Susan Ford

MALIA AND SASHA OBAMA IN THEIR FAMOUS INAUGURATION DAY COATS

CHARLIE TAFT WEARING HIS KNICKERBOCKERS

ACCORDING TO ALICE, THE BIGGER THE HAT, THE BETTER!

FIRST FAMILY PORTRAIT: THE FORDS
FROM LEFT TO RIGHT: MIKE, GAYLE (MIKE'S WIFE), PRESIDENT GERALD FORD,
FIRST LADY BETTY FORD, JACK, SUSAN, AND STEVE

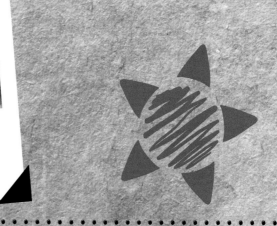

FIRST FAMILY PORTRAIT: THE CARTERS
FROM LEFT TO RIGHT: FIRST LADY ROSALYNN CARTER, PRESIDENT JIMMY CARTER, AND AMY (JACK, CHIP, AND JEFF NOT PICTURED)

The Spotlight Turns Ugly

Being famous opens the door for anyone to say whatever they want about you. Presidents have to deal with a certain amount of criticism and personal attacks; however, sometimes the meanness doesn't end with the adults in the family.

A Washington, DC, newspaper printed an article that stated a Secret Service agent stole a trophy and gave it to Amy Carter because she had finished last in a relay race at school. "Amy sat on the ground and howled," the story said. And when a Secret Service agent asked what was wrong, Amy cried, "I want a trophy." The story was completely false, and the president sought and received an apology from the paper.

Both Amy Carter and Chelsea Clinton were satirized on the popular comedy show *Saturday Night Live*. Amy's character made several appearances, often as a bratty daughter who complained to her father that he didn't have time for her. "It's always United States *first*, and Amy *second*!"

In one skit, Secret Service agents fed Amy answers to a quiz at school and beat up a student who called Amy a cheater. In a 1992 *Saturday Night Live* "Wayne's World" sketch, one of the characters made fun of twelve-year-old Chelsea's looks, implying that she would have a difficult time finding a boyfriend. First Lady Hillary Clinton complained, and the actor responsible for the scathing comment apologized. The joke was removed from rebroadcasts.

That wasn't the only time young Chelsea was made fun of for her looks. Early on during Clinton's administration, Rush Limbaugh, the conservative talk show host and political commentator, held up a picture of the Clintons' cat on his television show. "Socks is the White House cat," he said. Then he went on: "But did you know there is also a White House dog?" And he held up a picture of Chelsea. He later claimed he didn't mean to make that joke and that it was an accident.

"We really work hard on making sure that Chelsea doesn't let other people define her sense of her own self-worth. It's tough when you are an adolescent . . . [b]ut I think she'll be okay."

—Bill Clinton on his and his wife's attempts to help Chelsea deal with bad press

CHELSEA AND HER DAD, PRESIDENT BILL CLINTON, IN 1999

CHAPTER 3:
THE BEST PLAYGROUND AVAILABLE

Jesse Root Grant, the youngest son of Ulysses S. Grant, the Civil War general and president, recalled how kids from the neighborhood would flock to the White House to play baseball because it had "the largest and best playground available." Jesse, like many White House kids, investigated every nook and cranny of the mansion and found countless ways to amuse himself. With its many rooms, hidden staircases, and large reception halls, the White House was the perfect place to horse around, play pranks, make noise, and create mayhem.

"There's so much room to play—and a great big garden, too!"
—Caroline Kennedy

The Tyrants of the White House

In a time when children were to be kept strictly in place (to be seen and not heard), President and Mrs. Abraham Lincoln didn't much discipline their children and believed they should have free reign of the White House. "It is my pleasure that my children are free, happy, and unrestricted by parental tyranny," said their father. Yes, Willie and Tad Lincoln (their older brother, Robert, was away at college) were smart, funny, and a great comfort to their father during one of the most difficult times in U.S. history; however, they were also spoiled rotten.

Once, while exploring the White House attic, Tad and Willie discovered where all the cords for the house's bell system were located. (The president and first lady used the bells to summon staff.) Tad pulled on them all at the same time, making every bell in the house ring. Servants, Cabinet members, and secretaries ran all around in mass confusion, imagining the worst sorts of emergencies, until the president suggested someone look for Tad. There is no record of any punishment.

When an artist came to do the president's portrait, the boys snuck into the room where the painter kept his materials and squeezed out all his paints on one of the walls of the room. They then smeared their hands in the paint and spread it around. Again, nobody noted a consequence.

Once, the boys, along with some friends, put on a circus in the attic. Willie and a friend wore Mrs. Lincoln's clothes, and Tad painted his face black (which was a popular theater tradition back then, although it is considered offensive today). They invited the White House staff as well as Cabinet members, soldiers, and anyone else who could afford the five-cent admission charge. The boys sang "The Star-Spangled Banner," told jokes, and did some calisthenics. When the president's secretary ran up the stairs looking for Lincoln's reading glasses, he was not only surprised to find them on Tad's face, but also by Tad's reply when he asked for the glasses back: "Tell Mr. President he will have to pay and see the show if he wants his specs back." The president gladly walked up the stairs to the attic, paid his nickel, and watched the show.

THERE'S PLENTY OF ROOM TO PLAY ON THE SOUTH LAWN . . .
JUST WATCH OUT FOR THE HELICOPTERS!

WILLIE LINCOLN, SHORTLY
BEFORE HIS DEATH

WILLIE LINCOLN, THIRD SON OF PRESIDENT LINCOLN,
DIED FEBRUARY 20, 1862, AT THE AGE OF 12.
From a photograph taken by Brady at Washington, shortly
before the death of Willie Lincoln.

UNION SOLDIERS CAMPING
OUT IN THE EAST ROOM

THE WHITE HOUSE DURING THE LINCOLN ADMINISTRATION

With the Civil War going on, and soldiers even living in the East Room for a time, the boys' diversions quickly turned to war games. With sheets as sails and black logs as cannons, they transformed the White House roof into a battleship. They found an old telescope and kept a sharp lookout for Confederate soldiers. "Let 'em come," said Tad. "Willie and I are ready for 'em!" They collected as many neighborhood boys as possible and put them through military drills and dragged their father outside to review the "troops." The boys also staged riotous military parades up and down the White House hallways—complete with horns and drums.

And then, all too suddenly, there was only Tad. He and Willie both got sick in February 1862, most likely with typhoid fever, which was caused by contaminated drinking water. (Soldiers were using the river that the White House used for drinking water as a bathroom.) Tad eventually recovered, but Willie died. With his grief-stricken mother refusing to leave her room and his father having to move beyond his sadness to concentrate on the war, Tad was often alone. He was still unmanageable, but the tone of his antics changed. He became very aware of other people's suffering, especially his father's. So, while he was accused of hammering nails into the president's secretary's desk, he also demanded that the White House feed a bunch of "poor, dirty, hungry street urchins" he had found while out exploring.

Tad would also keep track of the people in line waiting to meet with his father. If he didn't like the looks of someone, he'd tell them they had no chance to see the president. Tad brought one woman to the front of the line when he heard that she was trying to get her sick son released from the army. While the rest of the line complained, the president met with the woman and personally signed the release papers. Other times, Tad would set up a table by the main entrance and sell refreshments, hinting that a nickel would go a long way toward spending a moment with the president. Tad raked in the dough and either used it to fund his next venture or donated it to the war effort.

Tad also spent time with the soldiers guarding the city. He would stand in line with them when it was "chow time," and then send boxes of gifts to the men. He was even made an honorary cavalry soldier, complete with miniature uniform and blunt sword. (His father said no when he asked for a gun.) When a photographer came to take the president's picture, Tad had his own picture taken in his military uniform. When the photograph was delivered, Tad drew a mustache on himself.

Whenever possible, father and son were together. Lincoln allowed Tad to interrupt important meetings, even if only for small matters. The president canceled war counsels with generals when Tad wanted to go for a carriage ride. (No wonder one of Tad's nicknames was the Tyrant of the White House!) One of their great joys was going to a toy store in town, where the president would buy just about anything his little boy wanted. Tad often remained in the president's office when he worked late into the night. They were both lonely, but they had each other.

After the war was all but declared over, with the president due to give a nighttime speech, Tad ran to the balcony where hundreds of people waited for his father and waved . . . a Confederate flag! A servant dragged him from the window. But before Tad could complain, his father stepped onto the balcony and read his speech, dropping the pages after he was done with them. Tad crept on his hands and knees, picking up the pages, whispering loudly, "Come, give me another," as he pulled on his father's pant leg. It would be President Abraham Lincoln's last speech before being assassinated five days later.

"If there was any motto or slogan of the White House during the early years of the Lincolns' occupancy, it was this: 'Let the children have a good time.'"

—Julia Taft, Tad and Willie's babysitter

TAD IN UNIFORM

IMAGINE LIVING IN THE WHITE HOUSE WHEN . . . THE CIVIL WAR WAS RAGING

THE WHITE HOUSE DURING LINCOLN'S PRESIDENCY HAD THIRTY-ONE ROOMS PLUS SEVERAL OUTBUILDINGS AND STABLES. MOST OF THE ROOMS ON THE FIRST FLOOR WERE OPEN TO ANY VISITOR AT ANY TIME OF DAY OR NIGHT. AN ELDERLY DOORKEEPER WAS SUPPOSED TO STOP STRAY VISITORS FROM ENTERING, BUT HE WAS OFTEN NOT AT HIS POST. ON THE SECOND FLOOR, NEARLY HALF THE ROOMS WERE OPEN TO THE PUBLIC. LINCOLN PUT UP A DIVIDER BETWEEN THE PUBLIC AND PRIVATE ROOMS ON THE SECOND FLOOR TO TRY TO GET SOME PRIVACY FOR HIS FAMILY. THIS PROVED DIFFICULT, BECAUSE THE PRESIDENT WAS BESIEGED DAILY BY OFFICE-SEEKERS (PEOPLE SEEKING GOVERNMENT JOBS OR FAVORS). LINCOLN'S SECRETARY JOHN G. NICOLAY SAID THAT THE EXECUTIVE MANSION WAS AN "ILL-KEPT AND DIRTY RICKETY CONCERN . . . I WONDER HOW MUCH LONGER A GREAT NATION, AS OURS IS, WILL COMPEL ITS RULER TO LIVE IN SUCH A SMALL AND DILAPIDATED OLD SHANTY." FIRST LADY MARY TODD LINCOLN SPENT A LOT OF MONEY TRYING TO FIX UP THE BUILDING, BUT IT WAS DIFFICULT, ESPECIALLY WHEN SOLDIERS WERE SENT TO THE EAST ROOM TO SET UP CAMP FOR A TIME.

WHEN TAD GOT SPANKED

THERE ARE A FEW ACCOUNTS OF TAD RECEIVING DISCIPLINE FROM HIS FATHER. IN ONE INCIDENT, TAD TURNED A GARDEN HOSE ON SOME STATE OFFICIALS AND ARMY OFFICERS. AND EVEN THOUGH THE PRESIDENT PROBABLY THOUGHT THE INCIDENT HUMOROUS, THE YOUNG BOY WAS SPANKED.

FIRST PERSON

JOURNALIST NOAH BROOKS SPENT A LOT OF TIME AT THE WHITE HOUSE DURING THE LINCOLN ADMINISTRATION AND WROTE OF THE DAILY LIFE OF THE PRESIDENT AND HIS FAMILY. THIS PASSAGE IS FROM HIS BOOK *WASHINGTON IN LINCOLN'S TIME*.

VERY SOON AFTER HE BEGAN LIFE IN THE WHITE HOUSE, TAD LEARNED WHAT AN OFFICE-SEEKER WAS. ALL DAY LONG, UNLESS THE PRESIDENT WAS ABSENT FROM THE BUILDING, THE OFFICE-SEEKERS LINED THE UPPER CORRIDORS AND PASSAGES; AND SOMETIMES THE LINES EXTENDED ALL THE WAY DOWN THE STAIRS AND NEARLY TO THE MAIN ENTRANCE. WHEN OTHER DIVERSIONS FAILED HIM, TAD LIKED TO GO AROUND AMONG THESE WAITING PLACE-HUNTERS AND INSTITUTE INQUIRIES ON HIS OWN ACCOUNT. HE WOULD ASK WHAT THEY WANTED, HOW LONG THEY HAD BEEN THERE, AND HOW MUCH LONGER THEY PROPOSED TO WAIT. SOME OF THE MEN CAME DAY AFTER DAY . . . WITH THESE TAD BECAME ACQUAINTED, AND TO THEM HE WOULD GIVE MUCH SYMPATHETIC ADVICE IN HIS OWN WHIMSICAL BUT SINCERE WAY. ONCE HE MOUNTED GUARD AT THE FOOT OF THE PUBLIC STAIRCASE, AND EXACTED A TOLL OF ALL WHO PASSED UP. "FIVE CENTS FOR THE BENEFIT OF THE SANITARY FUND," HE EXPLAINED TO THE VISITORS, WHO WERE NOT UNWILLING TO HAVE A FRIEND AT COURT FOR SO SMALL A PRICE.

Game Time

What games, sports, and other activities do White House kids enjoy? You name it!

✷ ✷ ✷

On Christmas Day 1835, Andrew Jackson threw a party for his White House kids, along with nearly a hundred guests—all children of politicians and officials. In the East Room they played blind man's bluff, hide-and-go-seek (in which a small item was hidden and had to be found), and spin the plate (in which a plate was spun on its edge and one player needed to catch the plate before it fell). When Vice President Martin Van Buren failed to catch a plate, he had to stand on one leg and sing:

> Here I stand, all ragged and dirty.
> If you don't come kiss me,
> I'll run like a turkey.

No one kissed him, and he was forced to strut around the room like a turkey!

As the children ran about, the Marine Band played, and then the kids all ran to the East Room for candy and chocolate, including "starch-coated cotton, each one enclosing a French pop-kiss," which the kids were invited to throw at one another like snowballs before eating the chocolate inside.

✷ ✷ ✷

Abraham Lincoln liked to wrestle with his two younger sons and their two playmates. Their friends' older sister wrote that "President Lincoln liked to play with the boys whenever he had a little time from his duties. Once I heard a terrible racket in another room, and opening the door . . . beheld the President lying on the floor, with the four boys trying to hold him down. Willie and Bud [Willie's friend] had hold of his hands, Holly [Bud's brother] and Tad sprawled over his feet and legs, while the broad grin of Mr. Lincoln's face was evidence that he was enjoying himself hugely. As soon as the boys saw my face at the door, Tad called, 'Julie, come quick and sit on his stomach.'"

HON. MARTIN VAN BUREN,

MARTIN VAN BUREN HAD TO RUN
AROUND THE ROOM LIKE A TURKEY.

WHAT'S THE MARINE BAND?

THE UNITED STATES MARINE BAND IS THE OLDEST PROFESSIONAL MUSICAL BAND IN THE COUNTRY. IT WAS ESTABLISHED BY AN ACT OF CONGRESS IN 1798 AND FIRST PLAYED IN THE WHITE HOUSE ON NEW YEAR'S DAY IN 1801. THOMAS JEFFERSON INVITED THE BAND TO PLAY AT HIS INAUGURATION, AND IT HAS PLAYED AT EVERY PRESIDENTIAL INAUGURATION SINCE, WHICH IS WHY THE MARINE BAND IS ALSO KNOWN AS THE PRESIDENT'S OWN.

The Lincoln boys liked to play a game that was a lot like baseball. Their father would often get a few at bats in before going back to his meetings. Jesse Root Grant also played baseball in a vacant lot next to the White House lawn.

Scott and Fanny Hayes loved forcing visiting dignitaries and senators to play hide-and-seek in different rooms in the house.

James Garfield and his children enjoyed playing billiards and croquet. The kids also raced their bicycles in the hallways and enjoyed the new lawn tennis court the president had installed. They only had a few months to enjoy their time at the White House, however, as their father was shot and died a few months later (see page 84).

Chester Arthur's young daughter, Nell, lived at the White House with two of her cousins. One of Nell's favorite things to do was to ride up and down in the newly installed elevator.

Teddy Roosevelt's six kids loved walking on stilts outdoors (usually through the White House gardens) and indoors, shooting water pistols in the East Room (until they were banned by the chief usher), roller skating, pillow fighting with the president, and whatever else they could think of. The boys and their friends liked to secretly follow the president around the house, mimicking everything he did in a game of follow the leader where the leader didn't know he was being followed. (See page 50 for more on the Roosevelt kids.)

THE PRESIDENT'S OWN IN 1864 . . . AND TODAY!

NOT MUCH IS KNOWN ABOUT NELL ARTHUR'S LIFE AT THE WHITE HOUSE BECAUSE SHE WAS SHIELDED FROM THE PRESS BY HER FATHER, WHO ONCE SAID, "I MAY BE PRESIDENT OF THE UNITED STATES . . . BUT MY PRIVATE LIFE IS NOBODY'S . . . BUSINESS."

✳ ✳ ✳

Charlie Taft and his friends played hide-and-seek in the attic and sardines in the basement. Sardines is like hide-and-seek, except that only one person hides and everyone else looks for them. When one of the seekers finds the person hiding, he hides with him. The game is over when only one seeker is left.

ON SUNDAYS, THE HAYES FAMILY WOULD INVITE SENATORS AND CABINET MEMBERS TO THE WHITE HOUSE LIBRARY TO SING HYMNS. MRS. HAYES SITS BEHIND THE PIANO PLAYER WITH SCOTT, THE PRESIDENT SITS AT THE TABLE, AND FANNIE IS ON THE COUCH.

✳ ✳ ✳

Amy Carter enjoyed roller skating, playing with her thirty-nine teddy bears, and bowling.

✳ ✳ ✳

Chelsea Clinton's parents would fly in her friends from Arkansas (their home state) for sleepovers. For Chelsea's sixteenth birthday, she and her friends took a bus to Camp David (the presidential vacation home in Maryland) for a party and a game of paintball. But this was no ordinary paintball session—it was planned and operated by the U.S. Marines!

Hoppy Easter

One game that is a tradition at the White House is the annual Easter Egg Roll that takes place on the Monday after Easter and is open to the public. The rules of the game are simple: Kids push a hard-boiled egg through the grass with a long-handled spoon. The first person to cross the finish line wins.

Historians argue about when this tradition first started; however, by 1876, Congress was annoyed that children had ruined the lawn around the Capitol building during an egg roll and actually passed a law protecting the grounds and

THE FIRST WHITE HOUSE ELEVATOR (NOT THIS ONE) WAS INSTALLED IN 1881. IT WASN'T ELECTRIC, BUT INSTEAD WAS OPERATED BY A STEAM ENGINE IN THE BASEMENT.

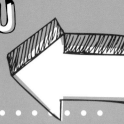
IN 2011, FOR THE FIRST TIME EVER, THE WHITE HOUSE EASTER EGG ROLL WAS HELD INDOORS DUE TO CONSTRUCTION. AND INSTEAD OF A ROLL, CHILDREN WERE INVITED INSIDE THE MANSION TO SEARCH FOR HIDDEN EGGS. THEY WERE HIDDEN ON ALL THREE FLOORS OF THE WHITE HOUSE. KIDS COULD ALSO PLAY LASER TAG AND VIDEO GAMES ON COMPUTERS PLACED THROUGHOUT THE MANSION.

banning future egg rolls there. Two years later, President Rutherford B. Hayes invited the public to roll their eggs at the White House instead. Fanny and Scott Hayes enjoyed the festivities, as have many White House kids since. Nearly every presidential administration has hosted the roll on the South Lawn, although it was held in various locations during World War II. In 1953, fifty thousand people attended the Easter Egg Roll at the White House, and so many kids (and some adults) grabbed eggs from President Dwight Eisenhower's grandson, David, to keep as souvenirs that the boy broke down in tears.

These days, tickets are issued for the event, and it includes music, games, food, souvenirs, and a visit from the Easter Bunny. In 2009, the pop star Fergie sang the national anthem, and each attendee received a presidential wooden egg signed by Barack and Michelle Obama.

DURING THE 1923 EASTER EGG ROLL, THIS WHITE HOUSE POLICEMAN WAS IN CHARGE OF CARING FOR ALL THE CHILDREN LOST DURING THE FESTIVITIES.

THE WHITE HOUSE EASTER EGG ROLL IN 1939

The Most Daring Stunts

Which White House kid performed the most daring stunt at the White House? Here are the candidates.

One day, Mary Todd Lincoln was entertaining a group of dignified women in the East Room when they heard a child yell, "Get out of the way there!" Tad rushed into the room in a goat-drawn chariot (Tad had harnessed his two goats to a chair), drove around the astonished women a few times, and then left.

Irvin Garfield, the eleven-year-old son of James Garfield, rode his high-wheeled bicycle down the grand staircase, sped into the East Room, and did a couple turns before, most likely, starting the ride all over again.

Teddy Roosevelt's children borrowed large tin trays from the kitchen and used them to slide down the stairs.

Quentin Roosevelt, Teddy's youngest son, attempted to cheer up his sick brother Archie by sneaking Archie's pony, Algonquin, into the White House, stuffing him in the elevator, and taking him to the sick boy's room—all without getting caught (or getting in trouble!).

Charlie Taft drove his mother's electric car (she didn't like the big gasoline "machines") into a tree, putting it out of commission. He also organized games of tag on the *roof* of the White House, which included sliding down the roof to a balcony below!

Although Woodrow Wilson's daughters were adults (all three in their twenties) when their father became president, their stunt deserves mention. Two of them posed as tourists and went on a bus tour of Washington, DC. As they passed the White House, one of the daughters said to the guide, "Oh, mister, can't we go in? I want to see where the Wilson girls sleep."

Calvin Coolidge's boys wrestled with lion cubs that their father received as a gift.

Lynda Johnson, curious about what White House tourists were saying, put on a trench coat, wore a scarf over her head, and joined a White House tour. She left with the tour and found herself outside the White House on Pennsylvania Avenue. Lynda had to convince the officer at the gate to let her back in.

Susan Ford, the seventeen-year-old daughter of President Gerald Ford, was jokingly challenged by a Secret Service agent to attempt to get away from the agency's constant protection. Susan hopped into her car and took off. Her mother was driving through the White House entrance at the time, and as the gates opened, Susan sped away before the gates could close. Susan drove around Washington for a while, picked up a friend, and had some fun before returning home.

ARCHIE ROOSEVELT AND HIS PRIZED
PONY, ALGONQUIN

FIRST FAMILY PORTRAIT: THE ROOSEVELTS FROM LEFT TO RIGHT: QUENTIN, PRESIDENT TEDDY ROOSEVELT, TED, JR., ARCHIE, ALICE, KERMIT, FIRST LADY EDITH ROOSEVELT, AND ETHEL

ARCHIE AND QUENTIN WERE HONORARY MEMBERS OF THE WHITE HOUSE POLICE FORCE. EVERY MORNING THEY WOULD LINE UP WITH THE POLICEMEN FOR EARLY MORNING ROLL CALL.

Running Riot

Teddy Roosevelt was one of the nation's most influential leaders, who believed that through hard work and living "the active life," one could overcome any obstacle. It is often said that he did more before nine in the morning than most could hope to accomplish in a whole day. At the time, he was the youngest president to serve in the White House, and he, his wife, and his children brought an excitement to the mansion that the staff and public had never before seen. The Roosevelt kids didn't just play in and around the White House; they nearly shook the mansion off its foundation! Six children accompanied their parents to the mansion in September 1901: Alice (seventeen), Teddy's daughter from his first marriage; Theodore, Jr. (fourteen); Kermit (twelve); Ethel (ten); Archie (seven); and Quentin (three). And like their father, each was rowdy, adventurous, intelligent, and noisy.

They explored the White House by climbing between floors and ceilings where no one had been in a hundred years. They found uses for rooms that hadn't been lived in for several presidential terms. They shimmied up the flagpoles, swam in the fountains, ran on the roof, and explored the attic and basement. When they played, they played hard, and the furniture and floors paid the price. Adults began to fear walking into the White House. Would Alice surprise them with her cap pistol? Would Archie wave to them from the top of the tallest tree? Anything was possible.

Nor was the surrounding neighborhood safe. Archie and Quentin, seeing the lamplighter climbing his ladder to light the gas lampposts late one afternoon, waited for him to finish one section and then scrambled up the posts and extinguished the lights. When the lamplighter finished another section, they waited for him to leave and then hit that section. A watchman finally caught them and was only persuaded not to press charges when he realized he had none other than the president's children in his custody.

Teddy Roosevelt was the first president to be given a turkey by the Turkey Farmers Association for Thanksgiving. However, when Quentin and Archie were seen chasing the poor bird with "swinging hatchets," they were criticized in newspapers for being cruel to animals.

Ethel was as rough as the boys. When the daughters of Washington officials were sent to the White House to play, they'd often arrive in fancy dresses. One dressed-up little girl asked Ethel if she wanted to play. Ethel, who had just been at the stables riding a new pony, responded, "Play? Play dressed up like that, while everybody would laugh at me? Go home and get on your everyday clothes, and then we'll play."

"One of the worst things in the world is being the child of a president. It's a terrible life they lead."
—Franklin Delano Roosevelt

"I think you are mistaken in calling me the first boy of the land since I have done nothing. It is my father who is president. Rather, the first boy of the land would be some boy who has distinguished himself through his own actions."
—Calvin Coolidge, Jr.

ETHEL ALSO HAD A QUIET SIDE.

As Quentin grew older, he became the most adventurous of the Roosevelt kids. He created the White House Gang, a group of boys who would find new and exciting ways to cause trouble. (Charlie Taft, a future first kid, was part of the gang, which gave him all sorts of ideas for when he had the run of the mansion.) One of their favorite games was Chase the President. The rules were simple: Lure the president up to the attic and then chase him around the White House relics stored up there until he was caught and brought to the ground.

The gang also enjoyed staging "attacks" on government buildings. One day, they aimed mirrors and reflected sunlight into the offices of the State, War, and Navy Building. Someone at the building complained to the president, who then sent a message to the boys: "You, under the trees, all of you. Attack on this building must immediately cease, halt, stop. Clerks cannot work. Government business interrupted. Report without delay to me for you know what. Theodore Roosevelt." Teddy then conducted a mock court martial and pronounced them all guilty.

The boys once nearly knocked over a giant 350-pound bust of President Martin Van Buren, and Quentin did manage to damage a full-length portrait of First Lady Lucy Hayes when he rammed his speeding wagon into it, ripping a hole in the lower part of the canvas. He thought he could fix it with a wooden board, tacks, and brown paint. Thankfully, he asked Eddie Norris, who worked in the boiler room, for help, and Eddie suggested to Quentin that the White House staff would best know how to repair the damage.

During a sleepover, Quentin and his gang members covered a portrait of Andrew Jackson with spitballs. They climbed on chairs and decorated Jackson's face with soggy lumps of paper: three lumps across his forehead, one on each of his coat buttons, one on each ear, and one for his nose. The president was not amused, and though not known for being much of a disciplinarian, banned the boys from the White House for a time. "They were four very sheepish small boys when I got through with them!" Teddy wrote.

Even tourists visiting the White House were fair game. One afternoon, a group of tourists in the East Room were startled when Quentin burst out from behind a large vase and yelled, "Boo!" His gang stifled giggles from behind the curtains.

All this behavior was actually encouraged and expected by their parents. Their father believed that kids should rely on their own imaginations—meaning that if left alone, children would come up with their own games to play and have more fun. He called it "running riot." He also made sure his children grew up strong and "manly" (even the girls). When a White House staff member tried to keep the children from playing football because they could get seriously hurt, the president was not happy. He glared at her and said, "I would rather one of them should die than have them grow up weaklings." He had other expectations as well: "If one of my boys was a bully, I'd try to thrash it out of him. If he would not defend himself against a bully, I'd thrash him until I had some degree of manhood in him. He'd require but one thrashing."

Some would argue that the kids were simply trying to keep up with and impress their father, who believed one should live life to the fullest and enjoy every minute of it. Teddy was known to have once played ninety-one games of tennis in one day, and each of his children sought his approval by proving they were as "manly" as he was. With a father like Teddy Roosevelt, that was no easy task.

"I don't think any family has enjoyed the White House more than we have."

—Teddy Roosevelt

ARCHIE GETTING READY FOR A RIDE AROUND THE WHITE HOUSE GROUNDS

LITTLE QUENTIN WAS ALWAYS UP TO SOMETHING.

THE LINCOLN BEDROOM IS SAID TO BE HAUNTED BY THE GHOST OF ABRAHAM LINCOLN.

Ghost Hunting

One favorite activity of White House kids is to invite friends for a sleepover to watch for ghosts. Yes, many believe the White House is haunted, not by one, but by several different ghosts. The most popular is said to be Abraham Lincoln, who roams the hallways and the Lincoln Bedroom. Charlie Taft often led expeditions to find haunted spirits, and Margaret Truman and Amy Carter thought the Lincoln Bedroom would be a great place to hunt up some ghosts; however, spirits have appeared throughout the house.

- The ghost of Abigail Adams has been seen in the East Room hanging laundry (see page 9).

- First Lady Dolley Madison once appeared to scold gardeners for attempting to dig up the rose bushes she planted a hundred years earlier. The roses are still there!

- Andrew Jackson has been sighted in the Rose Room, stomping around and cursing.

- Abraham Lincoln's ghost has reportedly visited First Lady Grace Coolidge, the queen of the Netherlands (he knocked on her bedroom door and she fainted), and several staff members.

- Willie Lincoln has been "experienced" in several White House rooms.

- President William Henry Harrison was spotted in the attic going through some boxes.

"The last night before we left [the White House], which I guess would have been the nineteenth of January, Luci and I decided to spend the night [in the Lincoln Bedroom]. And I thought it was very uncomfortable. I think the mattress felt like it was made for Abraham Lincoln, I think the mattress was horsehair, or whatever. Anyway, neither one of us saw any ghosts."
—Lynda Johnson

THE PRESIDENTIAL ZOO

Over the years, first families have brought pets with them to the White House—many, many pets—and sometimes the pets have become just as famous as the human family members. In fact, for a house that also acts as a museum, it's surprising how many winged and four-legged creatures have called the White House home.

✷ ✷ ✷

Thomas Jefferson's grandchildren had more than thirty pets to choose from to play with. They included birds, dogs, horses, and for a short time, two bear cubs.

✷ ✷ ✷

John Quincy Adams's grandchildren had to contend with the president's pet alligator, which he kept in the East Room. It stalked around and chased visitors.

✷ ✷ ✷

Tad and Willie Lincoln had several pets, including goats, dogs, horses, and rabbits. When the White House was given a large turkey to cook for Christmas dinner, Tad adopted it as a pet, led it around on a string, and named it Jack. When it was time to prepare the bird, Tad interrupted a meeting and yelled, "Father, Father, someone is about to cut Jack's head off!" Lincoln replied, "Jack was sent here to be killed and eaten for this very Christmas." "I can't help it. He's a good turkey, and I don't want him killed," said Tad. Lincoln wrote out an official reprieve for Jack, and Tad got to keep him.

✷ ✷ ✷

Jesse and Nellie Grant received a parrot from the Mexican ambassador. Jesse loved dogs, but tragedy seemed to befall all his four-legged friends. When Jesse was given a beautiful Newfoundland puppy, which he named Faithful, Jesse's father told the White House staff, "If this dog dies, every employee in the White House will be at once discharged." Faithful was very well taken care of.

✷ ✷ ✷

Rutherford B. Hayes's son Scott bruised his forehead when he fell off his horse on the asphalt in front of the White House. He also received a goat at the White House to join his two dogs, cat, and mockingbird.

KERMIT ROOSEVELT WITH ONE OF THE FAMILY'S DOGS

Baby McKee, grandson of President Benjamin Harrison, used to ride on a cart that was harnessed to his goat, Old Whiskers. One day the goat took off with the young boy. It ran across the White House lawn and onto Pennsylvania Avenue! The president ran after the goat and finally caught up with them. The Harrisons also kept two opossums named Mr. Reciprocity and Mr. Protection.

PRESIDENT BENJAMIN HARRISON WITH HIS GRANDCHILDREN IN FRONT OF THE WHITE HOUSE

TEDDY ROOSEVELT, JR., WITH HIS BLUE MACAW, ELI YALE

Of course, Teddy Roosevelt's children brought a whole zoo to the White House. Their animals included badgers, mice, raccoons, pigs, parrots, dogs, cats, baby bears, snakes, a one-legged rooster, a kangaroo rat, and horses. Oh yeah, don't forgot the spotted hyena named Bill. It was a gift from the emperor of Ethiopia, and the family taught it tricks and let it beg at the dinner table for scraps. Oldest daughter Alice liked to bring her snake named Emily Spinach to parties and receptions. When she got bored, she'd take out the snake and let it wrap itself around her arm.

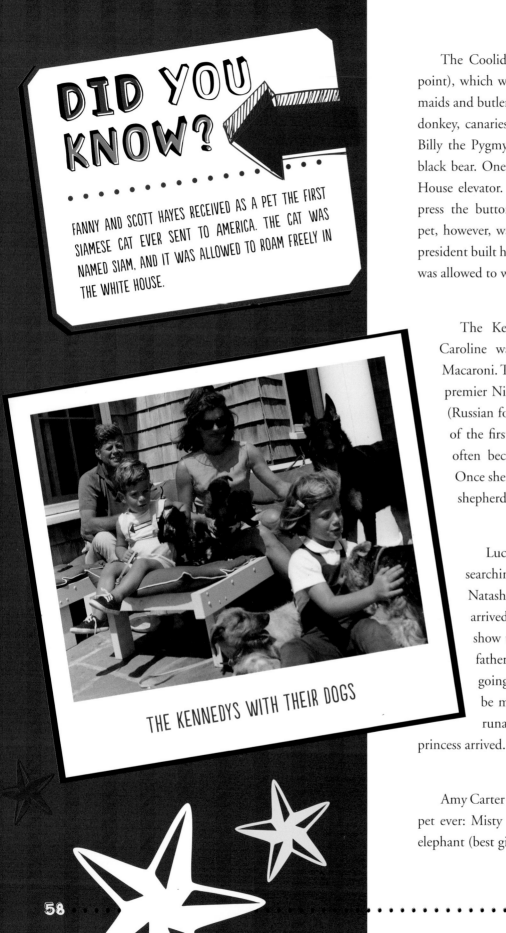
THE KENNEDYS WITH THEIR DOGS

The Coolidges had several dogs (up to eleven at one point), which would stampede through the hallways as the maids and butlers ran for cover. They also had Ebeneezer the donkey, canaries, birds, cats, Smoky the bobcat, lion cubs, Billy the Pygmy hippo, a wallaby, a small antelope, and a black bear. One of their cats was overly fond of the White House elevator. It would wait for someone to pass by and press the button to open the doors. Their most famous pet, however, was their raccoon, Rebecca. Cal, Jr., and the president built her a little house outside the mansion, but she was allowed to wander freely inside during the day.

✳ ✳ ✳

The Kennedys had many pets, including deer. Caroline was often photographed riding her pony, Macaroni. The young girl also received a gift from Soviet premier Nikita Khrushchev: a puppy named Pushinka (Russian for "Fluffy"), whose mother, Strelka, was one of the first dogs in space! First Lady Jackie Kennedy often became annoyed at reporters' silly questions. Once she was asked what Clipper, the family German shepherd, ate. She responded, "Reporters."

✳ ✳ ✳

Luci Johnson spent a weekend frantically searching for her escaped hamsters, Boris and Natasha, just before Princess Margaret of England arrived for a visit. "I knew they were going to show up on the floor of the East Room when my father danced with the princess, and there was going to be a lot of trauma, and it was all going be my doing," she said. Happily, she found the runaways in the kitchen pantry just before the princess arrived.

✳ ✳ ✳

Amy Carter gave her cat the best name of any presidential pet ever: Misty Malarky Ying Yang. She was also given an elephant (best gift *ever*!) by a Sri Lankan immigrant, but she wasn't allowed to bring it to the White House. Instead, she donated it to the National Zoo.

✹ ✹ ✹

Malia and Sasha Obama were promised a new puppy when they moved to the White House in 2009. The soon-to-be-president was asked what breed they were looking to get. He replied, "Our preference would be to get a shelter dog, but obviously, a lot of shelter dogs are mutts like me." It took several months, many news reports and press conferences, and even petitions from animal groups before their purebred Portuguese water dog, Bo, came to live with them.

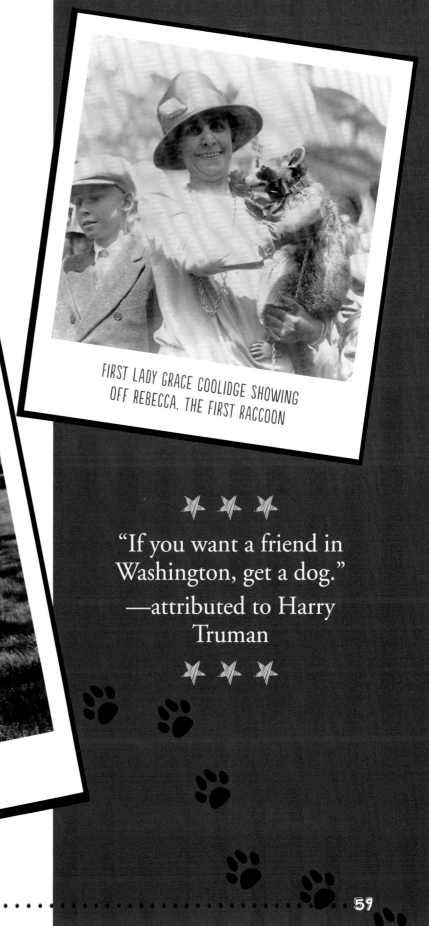

FIRST LADY GRACE COOLIDGE SHOWING OFF REBECCA, THE FIRST RACCOON

✹ ✹ ✹

"If you want a friend in Washington, get a dog."
—attributed to Harry Truman

✹ ✹ ✹

BO OBAMA AS A PUPPY

What about School?

The White House can provide great fun for kids, but how did they ever get their learning in? Well, some of them didn't, and the rest went to private schools, public schools, or boarding schools, or were taught at the White House by tutors.

Most early White House kids (before the 1900s) were privately tutored. They studied grammar, arithmetic, geography, French and/or Latin, and literature. They may have also taken piano, violin, or dance lessons, learned to knit, sew, do needlepoint, and more. Nelly Parke Custis, granddaughter of George Washington, was tutored by a Harvard graduate, who taught her to write. The president was pleased with her spelling, especially since at that time it was not considered something girls were good at! Washington himself also tutored Nelly in managing a plantation. He taught her how "to provide for the table and sleeping arrangements for any number of unexpected guests, but also how to manage servants." Nelly took harpsichord lessons from her grandmother, although Martha would often have to scold her fidgety, daydreaming student.

While Abraham Lincoln's oldest son, Robert, was away at Harvard, young Willie and Tad were tutored on and off at the White House. Willie was considered intelligent and a good writer, while Tad, who had a speech impediment that made him difficult to understand, had difficulty learning to read. After several tutors came and went—unable to work with the unmanageable Tad—the president said, "Let him run. There's time enough yet for him to learn his letters and get poky." And that was the end of school for Tad.

When Ulysses S. Grant personally delivered his daughter Nellie to Miss Porter's boarding school in Connecticut, he thought he had done a good thing. Nellie needed some discipline and focus, her parents thought. However, the

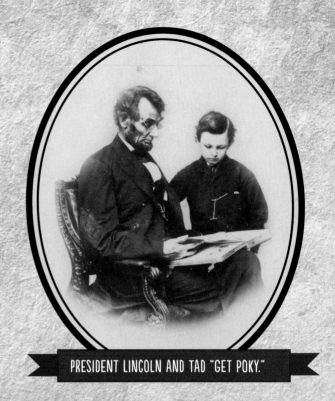

PRESIDENT LINCOLN AND TAD "GET POKY."

president began receiving telegrams from Nellie as soon as he returned from dropping her off, saying how homesick she was. Grant told her to return to the White House, and her education was replaced with receptions and all-night parties. When Jesse was sent to boarding school, he took a page out of his sister's book and also telegrammed, "I want to come home." Grant replied, "We want you, too. Come at once." Jesse returned to the White House, where he was way too busy for school. Jesse's lack of formal education did not prevent him from getting into college. His father boasted to a friend that "Jesse entered Cornell University . . . although he has never attended school but three years."

Mollie Garfield, daughter of President James Garfield, walked several blocks to school each day by herself. (It would be twenty-five years before Secret Service agents would be assigned to the children of presidents.) One reporter wrote that watching Mollie walk to school was "one of the prettiest sights in town." (It must have been a slow news day.) Her older brothers would lock themselves in the Queen's Sitting Room to study for their tests to get into college.

Grover Cleveland's wife, Frances, created a kindergarten inside the White House for her little girls and invited her friends' children to join the school. Jackie Kennedy did the same thing for her daughter, Caroline, seventy years later. She set the school up in the third floor Solarium, and the Kennedys shared the expense of the school with the other families invited to send their children there. President Lyndon Johnson allowed the school to finish the school year at the White House after John F. Kennedy was assassinated.

★ ★ ★

"Suddenly we became goldfish in a bowl."
—Eleanor Wilson

★ ★ ★

★ ★ ★

Schoolteacher: "So what does your father do for a living?"

Kermit Roosevelt: "Father? Oh, Father's *it*!"

★ ★ ★

"RED" AND "BILLY BUTTON" CARRYING THE PRESIDENT'S CHILDREN TO SCHOOL.—[Sketched by Theo. R. Davis.]

THE GRANT CHILDREN GET A RIDE TO SCHOOL

The Teddy Roosevelt clan did school in a variety of ways. Alice refused school of any kind and promised to do something terrible that would get her sent to jail if they forced her. The older boys (Ted and Kermit) went to boarding school in Massachusetts. Quentin went to public school (usually walking there by himself), and Ethel and Archie went to local private schools. Quentin was often in trouble at school. His offenses included "dancing when coming into the classroom, singing higher than the other boys, [and] drawing pictures rather than doing his sums."

Lynda Johnson went to college at nearby George Washington University. She complained that the noisy tourists outside her bedroom window made it difficult to study. She would often move her books to the quieter Yellow Drawing Room, while her sister, Luci, liked to work in the Treaty Room.

Amy Carter and her mother were once working on a term paper, and they requested some government data through her mom's office. Thinking this was for some government study, the staff sent over a truck filled with government reports and statistics. Bill Clinton sometimes relied on aides to find government research to help Chelsea with her homework.

✻ ✻ ✻

Sidwell Friends School, a private Quaker day school in Washington, DC, has been a popular private school for recent first kids. Malia and Sasha Obama are students (traveling each morning in an armored SUV with fully armed guards), as were Chelsea Clinton, Archie Roosevelt, Julie Nixon, and several sons and daughters of other Washington politicians. Hence, the school is good at understanding the security needs of prominent children, and White House kids don't stick out quite as much there, since many of the students' parents are also famous.

FIRST PERSON

MRS. ABBY BAKER, A WASHINGTON REPORTER, WROTE OF QUENTIN ROOSEVELT:

IF THERE IS ONE YOUNGSTER IN WASHINGTON WHO SHOULD LAY CLAIM TO BEING THE MOST DEMOCRATIC JUVENILE IN THE CAPITAL IT IS QUENTIN ROOSEVELT. WHEN QUENTIN IS READY FOR SCHOOL HE STRAPS HIS BOOKS OVER HIS SHOULDER, MOUNTS HIS WHEEL AND RIDES AWAY JUST LIKE ANY OTHER AMERICAN BOY. HE IS A PUPIL AT THE FORCE SCHOOL, ONE OF THE PUBLIC SCHOOLS OF WASHINGTON, AND WHEN HE ARRIVES THERE IN THE MORNING HE IS JUST "QUENTIN" OR "ROOSEVELT," AND THERE IS NO DISPOSITION ON HIS PART OR ON THOSE OF HIS FELLOW STUDENTS TO REGARD HIM IN ANY OTHER LIGHT THAN JUST AS A PLAIN AMERICAN BOY AND ONE OF THEIR SCHOOLFELLOWS.

CHAPTER 4:
THE PERKS AND PROBLEMS

If a White House kid were to write a pros and cons list for his or her life, it might look something like this:

PROS

Live in a mansion
Get my own room
House has a forty-five-seat movie theater
House has a basketball court, bowling alley,
swimming pool, tennis courts, and great big
lawn to play on
Travel around the world
The parties rock!
I'm a part of history
Free toys, pets, books, and more
Don't have to do any chores
—LIFE IS GOOD

CONS

Secret Service agents always around
Friends can't just come over to hang out
whenever I want
Can't ride my bike up and down the block
No privacy
If I do something embarrassing, it could end
up in the newspapers
Parents are extremely busy
The press says bad things about my parents,
and sometimes me
Like living in a fishbowl
—GET ME OUTTA HERE!

DID YOU KNOW?

WHEN A REPORTER WROTE A STORY ABOUT CAROLINE KENNEDY'S LOVE OF CHOCOLATE, THE WHITE HOUSE GIFT OFFICE RECEIVED HUNDREDS OF CHOCOLATE GIFTS, FROM HERSHEY BARS TO A SIX-FOOT, 200-POUND CHOCOLATE RABBIT FROM SWITZERLAND!

LIVING IN THE WHITE HOUSE IS DEFINITELY A MIXED BAG. THINK IT'S WORTH IT, OR WOULD YOU RATHER KEEP YOUR OWN LIFE?

The Family of Firsts

Sometimes it's good to be first. And when you're a member of the nation's first family, you often get to be the first to try out new stuff. Toy companies send you their toys before they're available to the public. (Whether or not you ever see these toys is another matter, since first families often return or donate gifts.) Book publishers send advance copies of their new titles in hopes some photographer captures you reading one of them, thus giving the book some free publicity. You get to see first-run features of movies before they're available on Netflix or on DVD without having to leave your home. The White House often gets the latest technology, and you may be one of the first kids to ever use it.

Thomas Jefferson spent many years in Europe before he became president, and he discovered exotic foods there that he later shared with his grandchildren. His grandkids were the first American kids to ever eat waffles and ice cream!

John Quincy Adams's children and grandchildren were early riders of a type of bicycle called a velocipede. It looked sort of like a bicycle, but it had no pedals. You simply pushed off the ground with your feet.

Fanny and Scott Hayes's father only served one term as president, but that was enough time for the two kids to do things no (or few) other kids had done before. In 1877, the first telephone was installed in the White House telegraph room. The phone was connected to the Treasury Department with wires. The kids would watch the secretary put through calls, and they were probably the first children ever to use a telephone. Their telephone number was 1. These are the same kids who owned the first Siamese cat in America and got to celebrate the first Easter Egg Roll at the White House!

THIS FORERUNNER OF THE BICYCLE WAS A BIG FAD IN WASHINGTON, DC, IN 1827.

"At times [living at the White House] seemed like a cross between a reform school and a convent."
—Susan Ford

Benjamin Harrison's family members were the first inhabitants of the White House to enjoy electric lights, long before most Americans could. However, they were afraid of them. Thinking they would be electrocuted at any moment, they made the White House staff turn them on and off.

✹ ✹ ✹

William McKinley was the first president to ride in a car, but William Taft and his family were the *first* first family to do all their traveling by automobile. (Taft got rid of their horse-drawn carriages.) And imagine fourteen-year-old Charlie Taft's excitement as he watched a Wright Brothers flying machine land on the South Lawn in 1911! (Since there were no airports in Washington, DC, Harry N. Atwood landed his plane at the White House to accept an award from President Taft.) Charlie was also one of the first children to listen to a talking machine (a phonograph).

FIRST FAMILY PORTRAIT: THE TAFTS
CLOCKWISE FROM TOP: PRESIDENT WILLIAM TAFT, FIRST LADY HELEN TAFT, HELEN, CHARLES, AND ROBERT

PRESIDENT TAFT'S MOTORCADE

Keeping It Real

Imagine never having to wash the dishes, take out the trash, make your own after-school snacks, clean up after your pet, or even make your bed or clean your room. White House kids have maids, butlers, chefs, and more to take care of many of the chores the rest of us need to do every day. But is that such a good thing? The kids may have thought so, but not all presidential parents agree.

President Andrew Johnson, obviously not worried about his personal safety (even though he rose to the presidency after the assassination of Abraham Lincoln), liked to keep it real by taking his teenage son and five young grandchildren on picnics—without any bodyguards. Apparently people either didn't recognize the nation's leader or they knew to leave him alone. He also loved going to Rock Creek Park, where they would all play in the water and skip stones.

Nellie Grant didn't much care for school. When her school kept her late until she completed her homework (the White House carriage had to call on her three times before she was allowed to leave), her mother called on the school's headmistress—not to complain, but to thank her for not bending the rules for Nellie. "Teach her she is plain, simple Nellie Grant, entitled to no special privileges," Julia said.

In 1962, First Lady Jackie Kennedy wanted a normal Halloween. She and her sister decided to dress as ghosts and take their children trick-or-treating in nearby Georgetown. The disguises worked perfectly, but it was difficult to remain anonymous with two Secret Service agents lurking nearby as they went from house to house. When Barack Obama was running for president in 2008, he tried to perform the simple task of walking his daughter Sasha to a Halloween party. They were quickly surrounded by photographers. "All right, guys, that's enough," Obama said at one point, before crossing the street and then running to get away.

Lyndon Johnson fined family members a dollar if any of them left a light on in the White House.

Even with all the staff to take care of every need, Chelsea Clinton had to clean her own room and sweep the popcorn off the floor of the White House theater after a night of watching movies with friends. Chelsea's parents, wanting to keep things normal, tore apart a third-floor pantry to create a small breakfast nook, where the family would eat breakfast away from all the noise and mayhem of the rest of the house. No doubt the Clintons learned this from the Kennedys, who turned a bedroom and living room suite on the second floor into a kitchen and dining room—in effect creating a smaller home within the much bigger one. When it was time for Chelsea to learn how to drive, her father took time out of his busy schedule to teach her. Of course, they drove around in an armored Secret Service car.

Malia and Sasha Obama have to make their own beds, and they're not allowed on Facebook. Hoping to keep the kids grounded, their parents also have a "no celebrities" rule for their children, meaning that the girls are to be kept from meeting famous people. That rule must have gone into effect *after* their daughters got to hang out with the Jonas Brothers at the White House on Inauguration Day in 2009. After enjoying a White House scavenger hunt put together by the mansion's staff, they found the popular Disney stars at the end of the last clue. The brothers posed for pictures and played a few songs in the East Room for the girls and about fifty other young guests.

YOUR VERY FIRST NIGHT AT THE WHITE HOUSE!

IT'S YOUR FIRST NIGHT AT THE WHITE HOUSE, AND YOUR PARENTS ARE OUT CELEBRATING AT INAUGURAL BALLS. WHAT'S A KID TO DO? WELL, THE WHITE HOUSE CURATORS AND STAFF KEEP YOU BUSY WITH A SCAVENGER HUNT. THEY CREATE A LIST OF THINGS TO FIND ALL OVER THE MANSION. WHEN TWELVE-YEAR-OLD CHELSEA CLINTON MOVED INTO THE MANSION IN 1993, SHE AND EIGHT FRIENDS RAN THROUGH THE HALLWAYS LOOKING FOR "THE HIDDEN STAIRCASE," "A YELLOW BIRD ON A PICTURE IN THE RED ROOM," "WHERE IT IS SOMETIMES SAID A GHOST HAS BEEN SEEN," AND OTHER HISTORIC ROOMS AND ITEMS. MALIA AND SASHA OBAMA AND SEVERAL FRIENDS HAD THEIR OWN SCAVENGER HUNT ON INAUGURATION DAY 2009.

FIRST FAMILY PORTRAIT: THE CLINTONS
FROM LEFT TO RIGHT: FIRST LADY HILLARY RODHAM CLINTON, PRESIDENT BILL CLINTON, AND CHELSEA

FIRST PERSON

JENNA AND BARBARA BUSH, TWIN DAUGHTERS OF GEORGE W. BUSH, WERE IN COLLEGE WHEN THEIR DAD WAS ELECTED PRESIDENT. ALTHOUGH THEY DIDN'T SPEND TOO MUCH TIME IN THE WHITE HOUSE, THEY HAD THIS ADVICE FOR THE OBAMA GIRLS WHEN THEY MOVED INTO THE WHITE HOUSE:

IT IS YOUR TURN NOW TO FILL THE WHITE HOUSE WITH LAUGHTER . . . IT ISN'T ALWAYS EASY BEING A MEMBER OF THE CLUB YOU ARE ABOUT TO JOIN . . . OUR DAD, LIKE YOURS, IS A MAN OF GREAT INTEGRITY AND LOVE; A MAN WHO ALWAYS PUT US FIRST. WE STILL SEE HIM NOW AS WE DID WHEN WE WERE SEVEN: AS OUR LOVING DADDY. OUR DAD, WHO READ TO US NIGHTLY, TAUGHT US HOW TO SCORE TEDIOUS BASEBALL GAMES. HE IS OUR FATHER, NOT THE SKETCH IN A PAPER OR PART OF A SKIT ON TV. MANY PEOPLE WILL THINK THEY KNOW HIM, BUT THEY HAVE NO IDEA HOW HE FELT THE DAY YOU WERE BORN, THE PRIDE HE FELT ON YOUR FIRST DAY OF SCHOOL, OR HOW MUCH YOU BOTH LOVE BEING HIS DAUGHTERS. SO HERE IS OUR MOST IMPORTANT PIECE OF ADVICE: REMEMBER WHO YOUR DAD REALLY IS.

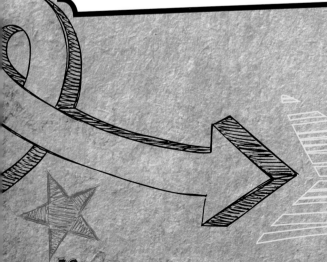

"I think it's hard enough to bring up children anyway, and everyone knows that limelight is the worst thing for them. They either get conceited, or else they get hurt."

—Jackie Kennedy

Jesse's Passions

Jesse Root Grant, son of President Ulysses S. Grant, had many hobbies, all of which were made more interesting and fun by living at the White House. Plus, since he didn't attend school regularly (see page 60), he had a lot of time on his hands.

When Jesse received a telescope as a gift, he didn't stick it next to an open window; his father had it installed on the White House roof for one of the best views in the city. Jesse would spend hours charting the night sky, oftentimes with his father. Jesse's mother would have to send a servant to the roof to tell them it was time for bed.

FIRST FAMILY PORTRAIT: THE GRANTS
FROM LEFT TO RIGHT: JESSE, NELLIE (ON HORSEBACK),
ULYSSES, JR., FREDERICK (STANDING), FIRST LADY JULIA
GRANT, AND PRESIDENT ULYSSES S. GRANT

"It's hard to feel at
home in a house
that belongs to 180
million people."
—Lady Bird Johnson

When Jesse was around thirteen, he and his fifteen-year-old cousin Baine Dent started collecting postage stamps. "The mania for stamp collecting came upon me with the thrill of a great discovery and for a time it held me in a fervor of enthusiasm that overshadowed every other interest," Jesse later recalled. It was easy to find rare and exotic stamps right on Jesse's father's desk. Once, upon seeing an advertisement in the newspaper offering a collection of foreign stamps for five dollars, the boys saved up their money for weeks until they had enough for the stamps. After several days passed and no stamps had arrived, Jesse decided to use the power of the White House to help him out. He started off discussing the matter with Officer Kelly, a member of the Washington police force assigned to the White House. Officer Kelly suggested talking to the president. Jesse's father asked him, "What do you wish me to do, my dear boy?" "I thought you might have the secretary of state, or the secretary of war, or have Kelly write a letter." The president invited the boys to the next Cabinet meeting to discuss it. (The Cabinet is made up of the president's senior officials who help him make decisions.) The next day, Jesse appeared at the meeting and told his story. The Cabinet members talked about what to do, and finally decided that Officer Kelly should write a letter. And he did.

"I am a Capitol Policeman," the letter began (written on Executive Mansion stationery). "I can arrest anybody, anywhere, at any time, for anything. I want you to send those stamps to Jesse Grant right at once." The stamps arrived a few days later, and both boys thought they had received more than their money's worth.

They also wrote to the American consuls (representatives living in other countries that help American citizens also living there) asking for stamps. Soon they were pouring in. This practice only ended when the first lady told the boys they needed to write thank-you notes to everyone who sent them stamps. That was simply too much work for the boys.

Jesse loved animals, especially horses. He received several pets as gifts from visiting ambassadors and politicians, but his favorite animals were two ponies named Reb and Billy Button. (Reb was captured during the Battle of Vicksburg in the Civil War and was once ridden by Tad Lincoln.) Jesse spent a lot of his free time with Albert Hawkins, the mansion's head coachman. "If anything could have made Albert unhappy, I imagine it would have been a day away from his horses," Jesse wrote later in life.

Jesse had tons of friends who came by every day to play. He decided to start a gang, which he called the K. F. R. Society. They met in the mansion's toolshed and planned what they would do that day. They even wrote and printed their own newspaper, the *K. F. R. Journal*. The boys would remain friends well into adulthood, and they even had reunions for years. No one ever revealed what the letters in the group's name stood for, although President Grant believed it was "Kick, Fight, and Run."

It's obvious that Jesse led a privileged life at the Executive Mansion. His father once commented on this when Jesse came down late for breakfast. "Jess, how is this? Nine o'clock and you just down to breakfast? When I was your age, I had to get up, feed four or five horses, cut wood for the family, take breakfast, and be off to school by eight o'clock." Jesse looked up, smiled, and replied, "Oh, yes, but you did not have such a papa as I have, you see."

Me and My Shadow

Want to go for a bike ride? Sorry. Not since Teddy Roosevelt's presidency have the White House kids been allowed to roam the city streets on their bikes. How about a movie with friends? No chance. You're better off simply requesting a movie from the White House staff and inviting your friends over to watch it in the downstairs theater. Walk to school alone? You gotta be kidding me! Wherever you go as a White

House kid, there are at least two men in suits and sunglasses talking into their shirtsleeves. Since William Taft's presidency, the Secret Service has been assigned to protect the president and his or her family. Over the years that has meant that once they step foot outside the White House, the kids have company . . . the armed and dangerous type.

The U.S. Secret Service agency used to be charged with investigating counterfeit money. After the assassination of President William McKinley in 1901, Congress requested that the agency also begin providing protection for the president. A year later, they took over the full-time responsibility for presidential protection. Today, they protect current and former leaders and their families, presidential candidates, foreign embassies, visiting world leaders, some Congress members, and of course, the White House kids (whether they like it or not).

SECRET SERVICE AGENTS

HOW MANY SECRET SERVICE AGENTS DO YOU SEE IN THIS PHOTO?

THE WHITE HOUSE ALSO HAS ITS OWN POLICE FORCE.

Called a "Secret Service nightmare," Barbara and Jenna Bush were both nineteen years old when their father, George W. Bush, took office. They were normal teenagers who liked to have a good time, and sometimes that "good time" meant trying to give their agents the slip. One time Barbara sped away in her car before her agents had time to catch up. There were also incidents when agents had to intervene, such as when the girls tried to get into a bar before they were old enough to drink alcohol.

Luci Johnson remembers resenting the agents' presence. "It's every teenager's mother's dream—and every teenager's nightmare." Her sister, Lynda, agrees: "It's like having your big brother on a date with you." Luci and her then fiancé snuck out of a party once to enjoy some time alone. When they returned and the fiancé said good night, the agent in charge, furious over the disappearing act, picked the man up by his jacket and slammed him against the wall, telling him what would happen if they tried something like that again.

Amy Carter may not have liked the Secret Service camping out under her tree house when she had her friends over, or telling her she couldn't go to her favorite ice-cream shop, but she was probably pretty happy to have them around when she was attacked, not by a potential assassin, but by a six-thousand-pound elephant! Amy was attending a pet show and performance when Suzy the elephant suddenly charged right at the first daughter. While spectators panicked, an agent picked up Amy, took off in the opposite direction, and leapt over a fence that Suzy soon splintered. The agent got Amy safely indoors while Suzy ran on until her trainers could control her.

Barbara Anne, President Dwight Eisenhower's twelve-year-old granddaughter, attended an all-girls summer camp. So did her adult, male Secret Service agents. They sat around campfires, helped with the cookouts, and by the end of the summer became the only male members of the sacred campers' club.

> "I ask you to consider the effect of saying good night to a boy at the door of the White House in a blaze of floodlights with a Secret Service man in attendance."
>
> —Margaret Truman, whose father would order the Secret Service to take her home if she broke curfew

When the Clintons wanted to go camping in Grand Teton National Park, agents had to find a secluded spot, stake out the perimeter, and patrol the area all night with night vision goggles. When Chelsea Clinton graduated from eighth grade, each guest at the ceremony at Sidwell Friends School had to be scanned by Secret Service agents with metal detectors. And when she went off to college, young Secret Service agents were used. They dressed like students and set up residence in a dorm room near Chelsea's. There are no reports of Chelsea ever trying to escape her security detail.

✳ ✳ ✳

When President Coolidge became worried about the distractions at college (the parties, the girls, etc.) and his son John's falling grades, he sent a Secret Service agent to act as John's bodyguard/babysitter/study enforcer. The fifty-year-old agent slept in John's room, but otherwise left him alone. "John was embarrassed and so was I," the agent wrote. "He decided to make the best of it and I made him realize I had no intention of sticking his nose into a book and holding it there." Still, having a Secret Service agent as his roommate was embarrassing for a teenager—especially back in the 1920s before all White House kids had Secret Service protection.

✳ ✳ ✳

When a first kid gets bored, sometimes he or she will play tricks on the Secret Service agents. Six-year-old John Roosevelt (Buzzie and Sistie's younger brother) once got into a Secret Service car and told the agent manning the vehicle that his grandmother was sending him on an errand. Since anything was possible with Eleanor Roosevelt, the agent took off. However, as Johnny's directions began getting vague and nonsensical, the agent realized he had been duped and took the boy back home.

SECRET SERVICE CODE NAMES

SINCE THE EISENHOWER ADMINISTRATION, THE SECRET SERVICE HAS USED CODE NAMES FOR PRESIDENTS, FIRST LADIES, AND OTHER IMPORTANT PEOPLE AND LOCATIONS. THE CODE NAMES USED TO BE FOR SECURITY REASONS, BECAUSE BACK THEN IT WAS EASIER TO INTERCEPT RADIO TRANSMISSIONS. THESE DAYS THE NAMES ARE SIMPLY A FUN TRADITION. (EACH FIRST FAMILY MEMBER'S CODE NAME BEGINS WITH THE SAME LETTER.) HERE ARE SOME FIRST KIDS' CODE NAMES:

JOHN KENNEDY: LARK
CAROLINE KENNEDY: LYRIC
LYNDA JOHNSON: VELVET
LUCI JOHNSON: VENUS
SUSAN FORD: PANDA
AMY CARTER: DYNAMO
CHELSEA CLINTON: ENERGY
BARBARA BUSH: TURQUOISE
JENNA BUSH: TWINKLE
MALIA OBAMA: RADIANCE
SASHA OBAMA: ROSEBUD

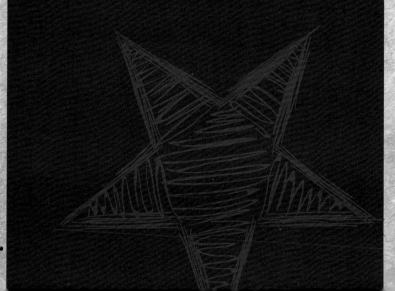

Presidential Peeves

Not all White House kids and parents got along. Here are some not-so-nice things presidents have said or written about their kids, and some of their children's complaints about them.

"My children give me more pain than all my enemies."

—John Adams, who held his children to extremely high standards that they could rarely meet

"I scarcely know my children or they me."

—Zachary Taylor, whose son, Richard, only saw his father once during an eleven-year stretch

"Scott begins to learn at last. He is not especially bright, but he is very much in earnest."

—Rutherford Hayes, regarding his son's progress in learning

"Father doesn't care for me, that is to say one-eighth as much as he does for the other children."

—Alice Roosevelt, in her diary

"I will never have to worry about either girl. Lynda Bird is so smart that she will always be able to make a living for herself. And Luci Baines is so appealing and feminine that there will always be some man around wanting to make a living for her."

—Lyndon Johnson, attempting to compliment his daughters. Lynda was angry because he made her sound like an old maid, and Luci was angry because he made her sound like she wasn't very smart. Way to go, dad!

"Don't you think it handicaps a boy to be the son of a man like my father, and especially to have the same name? I will always be known as the son of Theodore Roosevelt and never as only myself."

—Theodore Roosevelt, Jr., at age fourteen

"If I don't get out of here soon I'll have the willies."

—Allan Hoover, who didn't much like his time in the White House

THE ONLY PRESIDENTS TO NOT HAVE ANY SORT OF CHILD LIVING IN THE WHITE HOUSE WERE JAMES POLK, FRANKLIN PIERCE (WHOSE SON WAS KILLED IN A TRAIN CRASH JUST BEFORE PIERCE TOOK OFFICE), JAMES BUCHANAN (THE ONLY UNMARRIED PRESIDENT), WILLIAM MCKINLEY, AND WARREN HARDING. GEORGE WASHINGTON, JAMES MADISON, AND ANDREW JACKSON HAD NO CHILDREN OF THEIR OWN (ALTHOUGH JACKSON HAD ADOPTED CHILDREN), BUT THEY RAISED THEIR NIECES, NEPHEWS, AND WIVES' CHILDREN AND/OR GRANDCHILDREN AT THE WHITE HOUSE.

Calvin Coolidge, Jr., was working at a tobacco farm when he learned that his father had become president. A coworker said to Cal, "If my father were president, I wouldn't be working in a tobacco field." Cal answered, "If my father were your father you would."

WHITE HOUSE WEDDINGS ARE ALWAYS POPULAR NEWS STORIES.

Let's Party!

In 1975, the graduating class of Holton-Arms School in Bethesda, Maryland, wanted to have their senior prom at the White House. This sounds like a crazy idea except for one thing: Susan Ford was one of the graduating students. She asked her parents, they said yes, and the party was on! Two rock bands played while the teens danced the night away in the East Room. It was the only prom ever to be held in the White House, but it was by no means the only rockin' party at 1600 Pennsylvania Avenue.

✳ ✳ ✳

There have been twenty-one White House weddings, although only nine of them were for children of presidents. These weddings weren't just parties but, in most cases, national celebrations. Nellie Grant's wedding was called the greatest social event of the nineteenth century, and Alice Roosevelt's wedding thirty-two years later was called the wedding of the new century! People clamored for invitations to Alice's wedding and began surrounding the White House early in the morning, hoping to catch a glimpse of the bride. The White House was so crowded that several rooms were opened for guests, and at least two people fainted due to the congestion. Sixty-five years later, the eighty-seven-year-old Alice attended Tricia Nixon's wedding, held outside in the Rose Garden. She complained that her seat was wet, and probably had a proud moment or two as there were calls for a sword when it was time for Tricia to cut the cake (see page 21).

NELLIE GRANT IN HER WEDDING GOWN AND SITTING NEXT TO HER HUSBAND

To celebrate the end of Teddy Roosevelt's second term, First Lady Edith Roosevelt sent out six hundred invitations for a children's party. The kids feasted on creamed oysters served by the president himself.

Children's birthday parties could be grand affairs; however, Curtis Roosevelt remembers a birthday party with a lot of children, none of whom he knew at all! The press took pictures, they all ate cake, and then all the strange children left, and Curtis never saw them again.

During the Great Depression, the Hoover family sent out a Christmas party invitation that read in part:

> This is not like the Christmas parties you usually go to, where you get lots of toys and presents to take home, and very good things to eat.

FIRST PERSON

THOMAS PENDEL SERVED THE WHITE HOUSE AS DOORKEEPER THROUGH SEVERAL PRESIDENTIAL ADMINISTRATIONS, FROM ABRAHAM LINCOLN THROUGH TEDDY ROOSEVELT. HERE ARE HIS REMINISCENCES OF NELLIE GRANT'S WEDDING.

THE WEDDING WAS A GRAND AFFAIR. MISS NELLIE WAS MARRIED IN THE EAST ROOM RIGHT IN THE CENTRE OF THE THREE WINDOWS ON THE EAST SIDE. THERE WAS A BEAUTIFUL MARRIAGE BELL SUSPENDED OVER HER HEAD . . . PALMS AND OTHER PLANTS WERE ARTISTICALLY PLACED ABOUT THE ROOM. THE WINDOWS WERE CLOSED, AND THE ROOM WAS BRILLIANTLY LIGHTED. THE EFFECT WAS BEAUTIFUL IN THE EXTREME . . . THERE WERE TWELVE BRIDESMAIDS. ALL MARCHED DOWN THE GRAND STAIRWAY IN THE WEST END OF THE BUILDING, THROUGH INTO THE EAST ROOM. THERE WERE ABOUT THREE HUNDRED INVITED GUESTS . . . AFTER THE CEREMONY WAS ALL OVER THE INVITED GUESTS REPAIRED TO THE RED PARLOR; THAT IS, THE LADIES DID, AND I HAD THE PLEASURE OF PRESENTING TO THEM THE WEDDING CAKE.

DAVID EISENHOWER CELEBRATING A BIRTHDAY HE'LL NEVER FORGET

TRICIA NIXON WITH HER FATHER, PRESIDENT RICHARD NIXON, OUTSIDE THE WHITE HOUSE

But it is a party where you bring toys and warm gay sweaters or candy, or things other children would like who otherwise would not have much Christmas.

For Santa Claus has sent word that he is not going to be able, by himself, to take care of all the little boys and girls he wants to this year, and he has asked other people to help him as much as possible.

By all accounts, the party was a great success.

When David Eisenhower, grandson of Dwight Eisenhower, celebrated one birthday at the White House with a Roy Rogers Western-themed party, it wasn't enough just to wear cowboy hats. The famous Roy Rogers and his wife, Dale Evans, came to the party as special guests!

During large receptions, Teddy Roosevelt's kids would sneak a peek at the festivities from the top of the Grand Staircase. Then they'd start roughhousing and falling down the stairs. Their cover blown, their mother would shoo them back to their rooms.

When Caroline Kennedy did the same thing one evening, staring at the elegant gowns, sparkling jewels, and more, the conductor of the Marine Band, noticing the little girl at the top of the stairs, began playing "Old MacDonald Had a Farm." Caroline clapped and laughed, and then her mother invited her downstairs to dance and meet some of the guests while the band played more children's songs. From that time on, whenever Jackie heard the first strains of "Old MacDonald" from the Marine Band, she knew to look at the top of the staircase for her little girl.

O youth and health! O sweet Missouri rose! O bonny bride!
Yield thy red cheeks, thy lips, to-day,
Unto a Nation's loving kiss.

—From "A Kiss to the Bride" by Walt Whitman, who wrote the poem for Nellie Grant on her wedding day

EVEN DURING THE CIVIL WAR, THE LINCOLNS WERE EXPECTED TO GIVE ELABORATE PARTIES. TAD AND WILLIE DIDN'T ATTEND THIS CELEBRATION IN 1862 BECAUSE THEY WERE BOTH SICK. (WILLIE DIED SOON AFTERWARD.)

PRESIDENT TYLER'S PARTY FOR CHILDREN.

"A CHILDREN'S FANCY BALL WAS GIVEN AT THE WHITE HOUSE BY PRESIDENT TYLER, IN HONOR OF THE BIRTHDAY OF HIS ELDEST GRANDDAUGHTER. DRESSED AS A FAIRY, WITH GOSSAMER WINGS, A DIAMOND STAR ON HER FOREHEAD, AND A SILVER WAND, SHE RECEIVED HER GUESTS."—BENJAMIN PERLEY POORE, FROM *PERLEY'S REMINISCENCES*

There are many stories of White House kids having to make appointments with their parents' secretaries in order to see them. After the busy election of 1908, new White House kid Charlie Taft wrote to his father, "Could you please tell me where you are now and where you will be until Christmas? I'd like to keep a better track of my father." Caroline Kennedy once complained to her nanny that her mom was too busy to read to her. "Oh, Miss Shaw," Caroline said, "I wish you would come back on your days off and read to me. Mommy's too busy to read." Supposedly, Caroline Kennedy once woke up from a nightmare calling not for her parents but for her Secret Service agent.

The Garfield family complained when they realized they hadn't had breakfast together in nearly six months. And when the oldest boy, Hal, fell in love and wanted to talk to his father about it, he had to wait a month for a private conversation.

After his middle son's death, Abraham Lincoln made sure he spent time with little Tad, who was allowed to interrupt important meetings with a special knock the two had devised. If Lincoln heard the knock, he stopped the meeting and went to the boy.

One pretty cool perk of being a White House kid is that sometimes you get to travel the world. Both Nellie Grant and Alice Roosevelt were sent overseas on long tours, and both came back with souvenirs—and fiancés! Chelsea Clinton is also well-traveled. While at the White House, she went on a few long trips with one or both of her parents. She visited Zimbabwe, Tanzania, Uganda, Eritrea, Senegal, South Africa, Norway, Russia, Belarus, Pakistan, Sri Lanka, India, Bangladesh, Nepal, Germany, Italy, Ireland, Turkey, Greece, and Bosnia. Her mother thought it especially important to bring Chelsea along on her trips to third-world countries, because she thought that if it "changed minds in countries where daughters are not as prized as sons—well, all the better!" Chelsea met with world leaders, including Nelson Mandela, and visited places hit hard by war and poverty.

CHELSEA AND HER PARENTS EXPLORING THE GREAT WALL OF CHINA

PRESIDENT EISENHOWER NAMED CAMP DAVID, THE PRESIDENTIAL VACATION HOME IN MARYLAND, AFTER HIS GRANDSON DAVID.

Time to Ourselves

All Benjamin Harrison wanted was a quiet meal with his family, time to spend with his children, grandchildren, and wife. Like many presidents, he took comfort in having children around him, and he relished his time with his grandchildren. Imagine his frustration, then, as strangers wandered up to the dining room windows, peeking in and pointing while they were trying to eat dinner! Up until the early 1900s, the White House was more or less open to the public. You could wander the grounds and go right up to the house and, in many cases, walk right in and poke around. Frances Cleveland closed the gates to keep her young children safe (see page 18), and each administration since has seen security tighten more and more around the White House and its residents. Even so, the president and his family still have to go to great lengths to seek out some privacy for themselves, some time when they can stop being the *first* family and simply be a family.

When Jackie Kennedy wanted to take her kids out for some fun, she would disguise herself in an old raincoat, jeans, and a sweater. "I'm sick and tired of starring in everybody's home movies," she once said.

The Johnson girls were also annoyed by their lack of privacy. Lynda said one time that "the life of a family of goldfish is a secret compared to someone growing up in the White House." She also said, "Wherever we go, whatever we do, we may end up in the newspapers. I never have any privacy. I don't necessarily think I owe my life to the American people." Luci also had something to say on the subject when an interviewer asked her if she had a boyfriend: "I'd rather not talk about that, because although I'm the president's daughter, I also have a right to my own private life. Besides, whether I have a boyfriend or not isn't anything of national significance."

"There is but little privacy here, the house belongs to the government and everyone feels at home and they sometimes stalk into our bedroom and say they are looking at the house."

—Joanna Rucker, niece of President James Polk

"If you're alone in your room on the third floor, you have as much privacy as any kid who goes in her room and closes the door."

—Susan Ford

A reporter once tried to get Quentin Roosevelt to say something about his father. Quentin quipped, "I see him occasionally, but I know nothing of his family life."

History in the Making

White House kids get to watch up close as history is being made, and sometimes are even part of it themselves. However, turbulent times lead to unpopular presidents and first ladies—the very same people these first kids love dearly!

✹ ✹ ✹

Poor Peggy Hoover. Not only was her grandfather the president during the Great Depression, but she lost a good friend because of it. Peggy recalled, "A classmate once told me that she couldn't play with me any longer because, according to her mother, the Depression was my fault."

✹ ✹ ✹

When Luci Johnson's father signed the historic Civil Rights Act (which made racial segregation illegal) into law on July 2, 1964, she was doubly happy: Not only did she get to be extra proud of her father, but she also felt secretly pleased because this momentous occasion happened on her very own birthday. However, she also had to listen to antiwar protesters on Pennsylvania Avenue yell at the White House over the role of the United States in the Vietnam War. It could not have been a good feeling waking up to "Hey, hey, LBJ, how many boys did you kill today?"

✹ ✹ ✹

Not all White House kids are impressed with the history going on around them. People attending the annual Army and Navy Reception at the White House couldn't help noticing that President Teddy Roosevelt kept jiggling his leg as he shook hands with everyone waiting in line to see him. Upon closer inspection, they noticed two boys hidden under the couch the president was standing in front of, pulling at his pants leg.

✹ ✹ ✹

The assassination of a leader of a nation is a stunning and tragic event, made even more so if that leader happens to be your father. Four presidents have been assassinated while in office, and while many recall little John-John Kennedy saluting his father's coffin as it passed by after the president was assassinated in 1963, James Garfield's assassination was all the more tragic because two of his children witnessed it.

The Garfield family was just settling in to their new life at the White House in 1881 when the president, along with his two oldest kids, Hal and Jim, left for a trip to Williams College, where the boys would soon be attending. At the train station, the boys witnessed not only the assassination of the president, but of their own father. Jim was only fifteen

FIRST FAMILY PORTRAIT: THE JOHNSONS
FROM LEFT TO RIGHT: LUCI, FIRST LADY CLAUDIA ALTA "LADY BIRD" JOHNSON, PRESIDENT LYNDON JOHNSON, AND LYNDA

FIRST FAMILY PORTRAIT: THE GARFIELD KIDS
CLOCKWISE FROM BOTTOM LEFT: MOLLIE, JAMES, HAL (HARRY), IRVIN, AND ABRAM

PRESIDENT JOHNSON SIGNS THE 1964
CIVIL RIGHTS ACT. HAPPY BIRTHDAY, LUCI!

IT'S DIFFICULT GETTING TO SCHOOL WHEN ANTIWAR
PROTESTERS BLOCK THE WHITE HOUSE GATES.

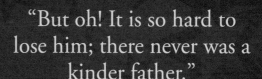

DID YOU KNOW?

ROBERT TODD LINCOLN, THE OLDEST SON OF ABRAHAM AND MARY, WAS IN CLOSE PROXIMITY TO THREE PRESIDENTIAL ASSASSINATIONS. FIRST, HE WAS AT THE WHITE HOUSE THE DAY HIS FATHER WAS SHOT. THEN HE WAS ONLY A FEW FEET AWAY FROM JAMES GARFIELD WHEN HE WAS SHOT AT THE TRAIN STATION IN 1881. (ROBERT WAS THE SECRETARY OF WAR AT THE TIME.) "MY GOD, HOW MANY HOURS OF SORROW I HAVE PASSED IN THIS TOWN," HE SAID. AND IN 1901, ROBERT ARRIVED IN BUFFALO MOMENTS AFTER WILLIAM MCKINLEY WAS KILLED. YEARS LATER, WHEN HE WAS INVITED TO ATTEND A WHITE HOUSE FUNCTION, HE MUTTERED, "IF ONLY THEY KNEW, THEY WOULDN'T WANT ME THERE."

years old at the time, and he later wrote in his diary, "I was frightened and could do nothing but cry. Hal was very brave and helped." It looked at first like the president would survive the attack; however, after eighty days, he succumbed to his injuries and died.

In the "Dad, please don't talk about me" department: President Carter got into hot water when, during a debate with Ronald Reagan in 1980, he mentioned that he had recently asked his daughter, Amy (then thirteen), about what she thought was the most important issue in that election. Amy had said, "The control of nuclear arms." Instead of praising Amy's intelligent answer, the press and Carter's political enemies made fun of the fact that he was asking his teenage daughter for advice. (Never mind that this wasn't the point Carter was trying to make.) This "Amy Speech," along with a whole slew of other incidents, helped send Amy and her family back to her beloved hometown of Plains, Georgia. (Her father lost the debate and the election.)

Tad Lincoln didn't often leave his father's side after Willie's death. He inspected Union troops with his father and even traveled to sites where fierce Civil War battles had taken place only days earlier. With the war at an end and peace at hand, Abraham Lincoln gave a speech in which he asked, "What shall we do with the rebels?" A man in the audience yelled back, "Hang them!" Before Lincoln could reply, Tad, who was right there by his side, shook his father's elbow. Tad said, "No, Father, don't hang them—hang on to them!" "Tad's got it," Lincoln exclaimed to the crowd. "He's right; we'll hang on to them!" Who knows what would have happened after the Civil War if Abraham Lincoln had lived and if Tad had had a few more years in the White House.

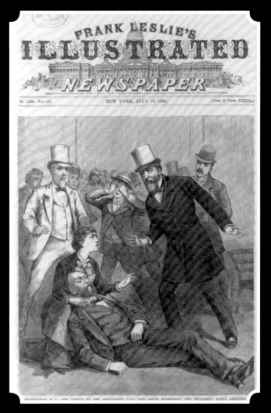

JIM AND HAL GARFIELD WITNESSED THEIR FATHER'S SHOOTING

MOLLIE HUGS HER FATHER

"The White House is more fun the younger you are. Later it gets more difficult. And you never get used to the Secret Service . . . Once you've been a White House kid, you'll always be a White House kid. It's always part of you. You'll always be so thought of even when you feel you're beyond it. You never get over such an experience, good or bad. Everything is compared to that experience before and after."

—Julie Nixon Eisenhower

Privilege or Problem?

History remembers the children, grandchildren, nieces, and nephews of the presidents of the United States. They were there when the presidents or first ladies needed to relax after a long day—a reminder of what is truly important in life. They were underfoot during the greatest speeches, sometimes squirming in their seats and stifling yawns. They watched powerful men and women make important decisions that would change the world forever, and then asked these same men and women for their allowance. And although their lives are a lot different from yours—showered with adoration, heckled with criticism, hounded for autographs and photos, and handed a lifestyle few could dream of—deep down, they aren't all that different from most kids. They laughed, cried, studied, pouted, suffered, played, and pranked like the rest of us. The only difference was the size of the stage their young lives were played out on. And whether they liked it or not, everyone watched. And we still do.

Knowing what you know now, would you want to be a White House kid?

"It was one of life's great privileges to be an eyewitness to history."

—Luci Johnson

"It was totally fascinating to live in the rarefied atmosphere of the White House for the simple reason that there was always something going on. The servants, the Secret Service, the staff. I loved every moment of it."

—Curtis Roosevelt

PRESIDENT JOHN F. KENNEDY WAS ASSASSINATED ON NOVEMBER 22, 1963. HIS FUNERAL WAS HELD THREE DAYS LATER, ON HIS SON'S THIRD BIRTHDAY. THIS STATUE IS ON DISPLAY IN DOWNTOWN RAPID CITY, SOUTH DAKOTA, ALONG WITH BRONZE SCULPTURES OF ALL THE PRESIDENTS.

APPENDIX A

And Then What Happened?

Here's a list of the White House kids presented in this book along with a short biography of their lives after moving out.

ELEANOR "NELLY" PARKE CUSTIS (1779–1852)

Returned to Mt. Vernon, the Washington home in Virginia, and soon married George Washington's nephew. Her first child was born a few days before the president's death. Had eight children in all (four of whom survived past infancy).

GEORGE WASHINGTON "LITTLE WASH" PARKE CUSTIS (1781–1857)

Went to college, served in the military, and built a home in Arlington Heights. Married at age twenty-three and had one child that survived into adulthood. His daughter married Robert E. Lee.

SUSANNA ADAMS (1796–1884)

Remained with the Adamses until she got married. Had one child, named Susan, and lived to the age of eighty-eight.

ELLEN RANDOLPH (1796–1876)

Remained unmarried for a while in order to study, travel with her grandfather, and take care of her family. Got married in 1825 and had six children in five years.

JAMES MADISON RANDOLPH (1806–1834)

Graduated from the University of Virginia and ran a family farm. Died at the age of twenty-eight.

MARIA HESTER MONROE (1803–1850)

After getting married at the White House, Maria and her husband moved to New York City, where her husband was postmaster.

JOHN QUINCY ADAMS, JR. (1803–1834)

After marrying his cousin, Mary, and making enemies of his brothers (because they both loved Mary as well), John tried to manage the family's business, but began drinking and became an alcoholic. Died at age thirty-one.

MARY CATHERINE HELLEN ADAMS (1806–1870)

Had one daughter (see below) and remained with the Adams family until her death.

MARY LOUISA ADAMS (1828–1859)

Married a cousin and died at age twenty-nine.

ANDREW JACKSON III (1834–1906)

Graduated from West Point and served in the Confederate army during the Civil War. Married a schoolteacher and had one son.

LETITIA TYLER (1821–1907)

Spent many years in a rivalry with her father's second wife, Julia Gardiner. Ran a girls' school in Baltimore.

ELIZABETH TYLER (1823–1850)

After giving birth to five children, died at the age of twenty-six due to complications from childbirth.

ALICE TYLER (1827–1854)

Married a clergyman and gave birth to two children before dying suddenly at the age of twenty-seven.

TAZEWELL TYLER (1830–1874)

Became a physician and served in the Civil War. Died from alcoholism at the age of forty-three, leaving an ex-wife and two children behind.

MARY ELIZABETH "BETTY" TAYLOR (1824–1909)

Was married twice but had no children.

ROBERT TODD LINCOLN (1843–1926)

Served as secretary of war and minister to England. Was also president of the Pullman Corporation. Married and had three children.

WILLIAM "WILLIE" LINCOLN (1850–1862)

Died in the White House at age twelve, most likely from typhoid fever.

THOMAS "TAD" LINCOLN (1853–1871)

After his father's assassination, moved to Europe with his mother for a time, where he went to school and actually became serious about his studies. Died at the age of eighteen, most likely from tuberculosis.

ANDREW JOHNSON, JR. (1852–1879)

Created a newspaper that failed and died at the age of twenty-six, leaving a wife but no children behind.

ELLEN "NELLIE" GRANT (1855–1922)

After her White House wedding, moved to Europe. Although she tried to make the marriage work, returned to the United States without her husband. Was ill and paralyzed during her final years.

JESSE ROOT GRANT (1858–1934)

Became an author, engineer, and world traveler. At one point, moved to Mexico and built a casino. Married twice and ran unsuccessfully for president.

FRANCES "FANNY" HAYES (1867–1950)

Worked for her father until his death, and only then did she get married. Had one child.

SCOTT RUSSELL HAYES (1871–1923)

Worked for a few railroad companies and died of cancer at age fifty-two.

HARRY "HAL" GARFIELD (1863–1942)

Became a lawyer, and then later president of Williams College. Worked in the Wilson administration during World War I, and received the Distinguished Service Medal. Married with four children.

JAMES RUDOLPH GARFIELD (1865–1950)

Also a lawyer. Was appointed secretary of the interior by Teddy Roosevelt. Married with four children.

MARY "MOLLIE" GARFIELD (1867–1947)
Married her father's secretary and had three children.

IRVIN GARFIELD (1870–1951)
Became a successful lawyer. Married and had three children.

MARY "MAMIE" SCOTT HARRISON (1858–1930)
Married and had two children. Did not spend much time with her family after her father remarried.

ELLEN HERNDON "NELL" ARTHUR (1871–1915)
Married, but died when she was only forty-three.

BENJAMIN "BABY MCKEE" MCKEE (1887–1958)
Worked in banking, got married, and had one daughter.

MARY LODGE MCKEE (1888–1967)
Married and had two children. Died at the age of seventy-nine.

RUTH CLEVELAND (1891–1904)
Was still a celebrity despite being kept from the limelight, and the nation mourned when she died of diphtheria when she was only twelve years old.

ESTHER CLEVELAND (1893–1980)
Married a British captain and had two children. Lived most of her life overseas.

ALICE ROOSEVELT (1884–1980)
Remained a part of the Washington social scene for several decades and was renowned for her witty and sarcastic sayings. Lived to age ninety-six—the longest living White House kid!

THEODORE ROOSEVELT, JR. (1887–1944)
Fought heroically in both World Wars. Served as assistant secretary of the Navy and governor of Puerto Rico and the Philippines. Served as a brigadier general in World War II, and General Omar Bradley called his fighting and leadership during D-day "the single bravest act" he witnessed during the entire war.

KERMIT ROOSEVELT (1889–1943)
Explored the Amazon with his father, fought for the British as a solider, and fought in both World Wars. Married with four children. He suffered from alcoholism and committed suicide when he was fifty-three.

ETHEL ROOSEVELT (1891–1977)
Drove an ambulance in Paris during World War I. Married with four children. Lived to be eighty-six.

ARCHIBALD "ARCHIE" ROOSEVELT (1894–1979)
Also served in both World Wars, awarded medals for each. Married with one child. Lived to eighty-seven.

QUENTIN ROOSEVELT (1897–1918)
Was a World War I hero as a fearless fighter pilot. Caught in a dogfight between two German fighters, he crashed and died at age twenty. His father never recovered from the shock of his son's death and died six months later. His mother said after his death, "You cannot bring up boys as eagles and expect them to turn out sparrows."

CHARLES TAFT (1897–1983)
Fought in World War I and later became mayor of Cincinnati. Married with seven children. Lived to age eighty-five.

JOHN COOLIDGE (1906–2000)
A successful businessman, married and had two children. Lived to age ninety-three.

CALVIN COOLIDGE, JR. (1908–1924)
Died at age sixteen while his father was still president. While playing tennis on the White House lawn, he got a blister on his foot, which got infected. He got blood poisoning and never recovered.

ANNA ELEANOR ROOSEVELT (1927–)
Worked as an educator and librarian. Married in 1948 and has three children and six grandchildren.

CURTIS ROOSEVELT (1930–)
Worked for several years at the United Nations. Now retired and lives in France. Married four times and has one child and one grandson.

JOHN ROOSEVELT BOETTIGER (1939–)
Was a professor for many years and wrote a biography of his parents' lives. Lives in Norway with his wife, and has four children and seven grandchildren.

MARGARET TRUMAN (1924–2008)
Started off on a singing career, but became a successful author. Married with four children.

DWIGHT DAVID EISENHOWER, JR. (1948–)
An author and college professor. Was a finalist for the Pulitzer Prize in history for his book *Eisenhower at War, 1943–1945*. Married to Julie Nixon (President Nixon's daughter) and has three children.

BARBARA ANNE EISENHOWER (1949–)
A decorator, businesswoman, board member, and wife to an Austrian billionaire.

CAROLINE KENNEDY (1957–)
Lawyer, author, and married with three children.

JOHN KENNEDY (1960–1999)
Worked for the district attorney's office of New York and created a political magazine called *George* (named after George Washington). Married in 1996, but he and his wife died in a tragic plane crash in 1999. He was piloting the airplane.

LYNDA JOHNSON (1944–)
Remained at the mansion after her White House wedding to a Marine captain while her husband served in the Vietnam War. Has served as chairman of the board of Reading Is Fundamental, and has three children. Her husband became governor of Virginia as well as a two-term senator.

LUCI JOHNSON (1947–)
Married at age nineteen and had four children. Divorced after thirteen years and remarried five years later. Is a successful businesswoman and has served on many civic boards.

SUSAN FORD (1957–)
Worked as a photojournalist and board member of the Betty Ford Center (a place for people who are addicted to drugs and alcohol), and is also an author. Married one of her father's former Secret Service agents in 1979 and had two daughters. Divorced in 1988 and remarried in 1989.

AMY CARTER (1967–)
Became known for her political activism and participated in several protests in the 1980s and 1990s. Was arrested during a demonstration in 1986. Married in 1996 and has one son. Keeps a very low profile and doesn't grant interviews.

CHELSEA CLINTON (1980–)
After graduating from Stanford University in 2001, studied at Oxford in England as well as Columbia University in New York. Married in 2010 and lives and works in New York.

BARBARA BUSH (1981–)
Worked with AIDS patients in Africa and is cofounder of a public health–focused nonprofit organization. Currently lives in New York City and works for a museum.

JENNA BUSH (1981–)
Married in 2008 and is an author, television correspondent, and teacher's aide.

MALIA (1998–) AND NATASHA "SASHA" (2001–) OBAMA
Both attend Sidwell Friends School and currently live in the White House.

APPENDIX B

The Presidents and First Ladies

#1 (1789–1797)
George Washington (1732–1799)
First Lady: Martha Washington (1731–1802)

#2 (1797–1801)
John Adams (1735–1826)
First Lady: Abigail Adams (1744–1818)

#3 (1801–1809)
Thomas Jefferson (1743–1826)
First Lady: Martha Jefferson (1748–1782); Martha Randolph (daughter who acted as first lady) (1772–1836)

#4 (1809–1817)
James Madison (1751–1836)
First Lady: Dorothy "Dolley" Madison (1768–1849)

#5 (1817–1825)
James Monroe (1758–1831)
First Lady: Elizabeth Monroe (1768–1830)

#6 (1825–1829)
John Quincy Adams (1767–1848)
First Lady: Louisa Catherine Adams (1775–1852)

#7 (1829–1837)
Andrew Jackson (1767–1845)
First Lady: Rachel Jackson (1767–1828); Emily Donelson (niece who acted as first lady) (1807–1836)

#8 (1837–1841)
Martin Van Buren (1782–1862)
First Lady: Hannah Van Buren (1783–1819); Angelica Van Buren (daughter-in-law who acted as first lady) (1818–1877)

#9 (1841)
William Henry Harrison (1773–1841)
First Lady: Anna Harrison (1775–1864)

#10 (1841–1845)
John Tyler (1790–1862)
First Lady: Letitia Tyler (1790–1842); Julia Tyler (1820–1889)

#11 (1845–1849)
James K. Polk (1795–1849)
First Lady: Sarah Polk (1803–1891)

#12 (1849–1850)
Zachary Taylor (1784–1850)
First Lady: Margaret Taylor (1788–1852); Betty Taylor Bliss (daughter who acted as first lady) (1824–1909)

#13 (1850–1853)
Millard Fillmore (1800–1874)
First Lady: Abigail Fillmore (1798–1853)

#14 (1853–1857)
Franklin Pierce (1804–1869)
First Lady: Jane Pierce (1806–1863)

#15 (1857–1861)
James Buchanan (1791–1868)
First Lady: Harriet Lane (niece who acted as first lady) (1830–1903)

#16 (1861–1865)
Abraham Lincoln (1809–1865)
First Lady: Mary Todd Lincoln (1818–1882)

#17 (1865–1869)
Andrew Johnson (1808–1875)
First Lady: Eliza Johnson (1810–1876); Martha Johnson Patterson (daughter who acted as first lady due to mother's poor health) (1828–1901)

#18 (1869–1877)
Ulysses S. Grant (1822–1885)
First Lady: Julia Grant (1826–1902)

#19 (1877–1881)
Rutherford B. Hayes (1822–1893)
First Lady: Lucy Hayes (1831–1889)

#20 (1881)
James Garfield (1831–1881)
First Lady: Lucretia Garfield (1832–1918)

#21 (1881–1885)
Chester Arthur (1830–1886)
First Lady: Ellen Arthur (1837–1880); Mary Arthur McElroy (sister who acted as first lady) (1841–1917)

#22 (1885–1889)

Grover Cleveland (1837–1908)

First Lady: Rose Cleveland (sister who acted as first lady until Cleveland married) (1846–1918); Frances Cleveland (1864–1947)

#23 (1889–1893)

Benjamin Harrison (1833–1901)

First Lady: Caroline Harrison (1832–1892)

#24 (1893–1897)

Grover Cleveland (1837–1908)

First Lady: Frances Cleveland (1864–1947)

#25 (1897–1901)

William McKinley (1843–1901)

First Lady: Ida McKinley (1847–1907)

#26 (1901–1909)

Theodore Roosevelt (1858–1919)

First Lady: Edith Roosevelt (1861–1948)

#27 (1909–1913)

William Taft (1857–1930)

First Lady: Helen Taft (1861–1943)

#28 (1913–1921)

Woodrow Wilson (1856–1924)

First Lady: Ellen Wilson (1860–1914); Edith Wilson (1872–1961)

#29 (1921–1923)

Warren G. Harding (1865–1923)

First Lady: Florence Harding (1860–1924)

#30 (1923–1929)

Calvin Coolidge (1872–1933)

First Lady: Grace Coolidge (1879–1957)

#31 (1929–1933)

Herbert Hoover (1874–1964)

First Lady: Lou Hoover (1874–1944)

#32 (1933–1945)

Franklin Delano Roosevelt (1882–1945)

First Lady: Anna Eleanor Roosevelt (1884–1962)

#33 (1945–1953)

Harry S. Truman (1884–1972)

First Lady: Elizabeth "Bess" Truman (1885–1982)

#34 (1953–1961)

Dwight D. Eisenhower (1890–1969)

First Lady: Mamie Eisenhower (1896–1979)

#35 (1961–1963)

John F. Kennedy (1917–1963)

First Lady: Jacqueline Kennedy (1929–1994)

#36 (1963–1969)

Lyndon B. Johnson (1908–1973)

First Lady: Claudia "Lady Bird" Johnson (1912–2007)

#37 (1969–1974)

Richard M. Nixon (1913–1994)

First Lady: Thelma "Pat" Nixon (1912–1993)

#38 (1974–1977)

Gerald R. Ford (1913–2006)

First Lady: Elizabeth "Betty" Ford (1918–2011)

#39 (1977–1981)

James E. Carter, Jr. (1924–)

First Lady: Eleanor Rosalynn Carter (1927–)

#40 (1981–1989)

Ronald W. Reagan (1911–2004)

First Lady: Nancy Reagan (1921–)

#41 (1989–1993)

George H. W. Bush (1924–)

First Lady: Barbara Bush (1925–)

#42 (1993–2001)

William Jefferson Clinton (1946–)

First Lady: Hillary Rodham Clinton (1947–)

#43 (2001–2009)

George W. Bush (1946–)

First Lady: Laura Bush (1946–)

#44 (2009–)

Barack H. Obama (1961–)

First Lady: Michelle Obama (1964–)

BIBLIOGRAPHY

Andersen, Christopher. *Sweet Caroline: Last Child of Camelot*, New York: William Morrow, 2003.

Angelo, Bonnie. *First Families: The Impact of the White House on Their Lives*. New York: William Morrow, 2005.

Anthony, Carl Sferrazza. *America's First Families: An Inside View of 200 Years of Private Life in the White House*. New York: Touchstone, 2000.

Atkins, Annette. *We Grew Up Together: Brothers and Sisters in Nineteenth-Century America*. Chicago, IL: University of Illinois Press, 2000.

Baram, Marcus. "Secret Service Slip-Ups: How Safe Are Our Leaders?" ABCNews.com, November 23, 2006. http://abcnews.go.com/Politics/story?id=2674373&page=1.

Brooks, Noah. *Washington in Lincoln's Time*. New York: The Century Co., 1895.

Carnwath, Ally. "Growing up in the White House." *The Guardian*, January 18, 2009. http://www.guardian.co.uk/culture/2009/jan/18/white-house-children-us-presidents.

Carter, Jimmy. *White House Diary*. New York: Farrar, Straus and Giroux, 2010.

Clinton, Bill. *My Life*. New York: Alfred A. Knopf, 2004.

Clinton, Hillary Rodham. *Living History*. New York: Simon & Schuster, 2003.

Cowger, Thomas W., ed. and Sherwin J. Markman, ed. *Lyndon Johnson Remembered: An Intimate Portrait of a Presidency*. Lanham, MD: Rowman & Littlefield Publishers, 2003.

Crook, Colonel W. H. *Memories of the White House: The Home Life of Our Presidents from Lincoln to Roosevelt*. Boston, MA: Little, Brown, and Company, 1911.

Donald, David Herbert. *Lincoln at Home: Two Glimpses of Abraham Lincoln's Family Life*. New York: Simon & Schuster, 2000.

Donelson Wilcox, Mary. *Christmas Under Three Flags*. Washington, DC: The Neale Company, 1900.

Dunlap, Annette. *Frank: The Story of Frances Folsom Cleveland, America's Youngest First Lady*. Albany, NY: Excelsior Editions / State University of New York Press, 2009.

Grant, Jesse Root and Henry Francis Granger. "A Boy in the White House Part II." *Harper's Magazine*, February 1925.

Hagedorn, Hermann. *The Roosevelt Family of Sagamore Hill*. New York: The Macmillan Company, 1954.

Heymann, C. David. *American Legacy: The Story of John & Caroline Kennedy*. New York: Atria Books, 2007.

Hoover, Irwin Hood. *Forty-two Years in the White House*. New York: Houghton Mifflin Company, 1934.

Keckley, Elizabeth. *Behind the Scenes, or, Thirty Years a Slave and Four Years in the White House*. New York: G.W., Carleton & Co., 1868.

Kessler, Ronald. *Inside the White House*. New York: Simon & Schuster, 1995.

Leiner, Katherine. *First Children: Growing Up in the White House*. New York: Tambourine Books, 1996.

May, Gary. *John Tyler*. New York: Henry Holt and Company, 2008.

Melanson, PH.D, Philip. *The Secret Service: The Hidden History of an Enigmatic Agency*. New York: Carroll & Graf, 2002.

National Children's Book and Literacy Alliance. *Our White House: Looking In, Looking Out*. Cambridge, MA: Candlewick Press, 2008.

NNDB. "Secret Service Codename." http://www.nndb.com/lists/050/000140627/.

Pendel, Thomas F. *Thirty-Six Years in the White House*. Washington, DC: The Neale Publishing Company, 1902.

Perley Poore, Ben:. *Perley's Reminiscences of Sixty Years in the National Metropolis*, Philadelphia, PA: Hubbard Brothers Publishers, 1886.

Perling, J. J. *Presidents' Sons*. New York: Odyssey Press, 1947.

Reit, Seymour. *Growing Up in the White House: The Story of the Presidents' Children*. New York: Crowell-Collier Press, 1968.

Roosevelt, Curtis. *Too Close to the Sun: Growing Up in the Shadow of My Grandparents, Franklin and Eleanor*. New York: Public Affairs Books, 2008.

Shellenbarger, Sue. "The Perils and Perks of Raising Children in the White House." *Wall Street Journal*, November 26, 2008. http://online.wsj.com/article/SB122765934554458413.html?mod=todays_us_personal_journal.

Starling, Colonel Edmund W. and Thomas Sugrue. *Starling of the White House: A Secret Service Man Who Guarded Presidents Wilson Through Roosevelt*. New York: Simon & Schuster, 1946.

Sweetser, Kate Dickinson. *Famous Girls of the White House*. New York: Thomas Y. Crowell Company, 1930.

Sweetser, Kate Dickinson. *Ten Boys from History*. New York: Duffield & Company, 1910.

Upton, Harriet Taylor. "The Household of John Quincy Adams." *Wide Awake, Volume 27*. Boston, MA: D. Lothrop Company, 1888, 363–377.

Vexler, Erica. "Luci Baines Johnson: Talks about youth, race, family, love and politics." *Ebony*, February 1965, pp 40-46.

Wagenknecht, Edward. *The Seven Worlds of Theodore Roosevelt*. Guilford, CT: Lyons Press, 2009.

Walsh, Kenneth T. *Air Force One: A History of the Presidents and Their Planes*. New York: Hyperion, 2004.

Watson, Robert P., ed. *Life in the White House: A Social History of the First Family and the President's House*. Albany, NY: State University of New York Press, 2004.

Wead, Doug. *All the Presidents' Children: Triumph and Tragedy in the Lives of America's First Families*. New York: Simon & Schuster, 2003.

Willets, Gilson. *History of the White House*. New York: The Christian Herald, 1908.

INDEX

Adams, Abigail, 9, 54
Adams, Charles, 9
Adams, John, 9, 77
Adams, John Quincy, 11, 56, 65
Adams, John Quincy, Jr., 11
Adams, Mary, 11
Adams, Mary Louisa "Looly," 11
Adams, Susanna, 9, 10
Algonquin, 48, 49
Arthur, Chester, 45
Arthur, Nell, 45
Atwood, Harry N., 66–67
"Baby Ruth and Baby McKee," 27
Blue Room, 11, 18
Brooks, Louise, 23
Brooks, Noah, 43
Buchanan, James, 77
Bush, Barbara, 15, 70, 74, 76
Bush, George W., 15, 30, 70
Bush, Jenna, 15, 70, 74, 76
Camp David, 32, 46, 80
Carter, Amy, 31–33, 36, 46, 54, 58, 62, 74, 76, 86
Carter, Jimmy, 31, 36, 86
Carter, Rosalynn, 31, 36, 62
Chief Usher, 19
Civil War, the, 40–43, 72, 86–87
Clark, William, 12
Cleveland, "Baby" Ruth, 18–19, 27
Cleveland, Esther, 18
Cleveland, Frances, 18–19, 61, 83
Cleveland, Grover, 18–19, 27, 61
Clinton, Bill, 30, 37, 62, 68–69
Clinton, Chelsea, 15, 30, 36–37, 46, 62, 68–69, 76, 82
Clinton, Hillary Rodham, 30, 36, 69
Coolidge, Calvin, 22–23, 76
Coolidge, Calvin, Jr., 22–23, 48, 58, 77
Coolidge, Grace, 23, 54, 58
Coolidge, John, 22–23, 76
Cooper, George, 27
Custis, George "Little Wash" Washington Parke, 8, 15
Custis, Mary Parke, 8
Custis, Nelly Parke, 8, 15, 60
Dent, Baine, 72
Donelson, Emily, 13
Donelson, Jackson, 13

Donelson, John, 13
Donelson, Mary, 13, 14
Donelson, Rachel, 13
East Room, 9, 40, 43, 44, 45, 48, 52, 54, 68
Easter Egg Roll, 46–47, 65
Eisenhower, Barbara Anne, 74–75
Eisenhower, David, 47, 79, 80, 82
Eisenhower, Dwight D., 47, 74, 80
Evans, Dale, 79
Fashion, 34–35
Flappers, 23
Ford, Betty, 35
Ford, Gerald, 34, 48
Ford, Susan, 34, 48, 76, 78, 83
Games, 44–46
Garfield, Hal, 82, 84–86
Garfield, Irvin, 48, 49, 84
Garfield, James, 45, 48, 60, 84–86
Garfield, Jim, 84–86
Garfield, Mollie, 60, 84–86
Geibel, Adam, 27
Ghosts, 54–55
Gouverneur, Samuel Lawrence, 11
Grant, Frederick, 71
Grant, Jesse Root, 15, 38, 45, 56, 60, 70–72
Grant, Julia, 15, 68, 71
Grant, Nellie, 15, 56, 60, 68, 71, 78, 82
Grant, Ulysses S., 38, 60, 70–72
Grant, Ulysses S., Jr., 71
Great Depression, the, 24, 84
Guiteau, Charles, 85
Harding, Warren, 22, 77
Harrison, Benjamin, 17, 57, 66, 83–84
Harrison, Mrs. Russell, 17
Harrison, William Henry, 14, 54
Hayes, Fanny, 45, 46, 47, 58, 64–65
Hayes, Lucy, 46, 52
Hayes, Rutherford B., 46, 47, 56–57, 77
Hayes, Scott, 45, 46, 47, 56–57, 58, 64–65, 77
Hoban, James, 9
Hoover, Allan, 77
Hoover Herbert, 79–80
Hoover, Irwin "Ike" Hood, 19
Hoover, Peggy, 84
Jackson, Andrew, 13–14, 44, 52, 53, 54
Jackson, Andrew, Jr., 13, 77
Jackson, Andrew III, 13
Jackson, Rachel, 13

Jefferson, Thomas, 11, 12–13, 44, 56, 65
Johnson, Andrew, 68
Johnson, Lady Bird, 28, 84
Johnson, Luci, 28–29, 54, 58, 62, 74, 76, 77, 84–85, 87
Johnson, Lynda, 28–29, 48, 54, 62, 74, 76, 77, 83–84
Johnson, Lyndon, 28, 61, 68, 77, 84–85
K.F.R. Society, 72
Kennedy, Caroline, 26, 31, 38, 61, 63, 76, 80–81
Kennedy, Jackie, 26, 58, 61, 68, 70, 83
Kennedy, John F., 26, 30–31, 88
Kennedy, John F., Jr. "John-John," 26, 28, 76, 84, 88
Khrushchev, Nikita, 58
Knickerbockers, 34
Lee, Robert E., 8
Lewis and Clark Expedition, 12
Lewis, Meriwether, 12
Limbaugh, Rush, 36
Lincoln bedroom, 54
Lincoln, Abraham, 16, 30, 38–43, 44–45, 54–55, 56, 60, 68, 82, 86–87
Lincoln, Mary Todd, 16–17, 38, 48, 87
Lincoln, Robert, 16, 38, 60, 85
Lincoln, Thomas "Tad," 16–17, 38–43, 44, 48, 56, 60, 72, 77, 82, 86–87
Lincoln, William "Willie," 16–17, 38–40, 44, 54, 56, 60, 77
Longworth, Nicholas, 21
Madison, Dolley, 54
Madison, James, 77
Marine Band, the, 44–45, 80–81
McKee, Benjamin "Baby McKee," 17, 27, 57
McKee, Marthena, 17
McKee, Mary Harrison, 17
McKee, Mary Lodge, 17
McKinley, William, 20, 66, 73, 77, 85
McQueen, Steve, 28–29
Monroe, James, 11
Monroe, Maria Hester, 11
New Deal, the, 24
Nicolay, John G., 43
Nixon, Julie, 62
Nixon, Tricia, 78, 79
Norris, Eddie, 52
Obama, Barack, 30–31, 47, 68
Obama, Bo, 59

Obama, Malia, 5, 15, 30–31, 32, 34, 59, 62, 69, 76

Obama, Michelle, 30–31, 47

Obama, Sasha, 5, 15, 30–31, 34, 59, 62, 69, 76

Parties, 78–80

Pendel, Thomas, 79

Pennsylvania Avenue, 4, 9, 16, 48, 57, 85

Pets, 56–59

Pierce, Franklin, 77

Polk, James, 77, 83

Poore, Benjamin Perley, 82

Randolph, James Madison, 11

Randolph, Martha Jefferson, 11

Reagan, Ronald, 86

Roaring Twenties, the, 23

Rogers, Roy, 79

Roosevelt, Alice, 20–22, 34–35, 50, 62, 77, 78, 82

Roosevelt, Anna Eleanor "Sistie," 24–25, 76

Roosevelt, Archie, 48, 49, 50–53, 62

Roosevelt, Curtis "Buzzie," 24–25, 46, 76, 79

Roosevelt, Edith, 50, 79

Roosevelt, Eleanor, 24–25

Roosevelt, Ethel, 50–51, 62

Roosevelt, Franklin Delano, 24–25, 46

Roosevelt, Johnny, 25, 76

Roosevelt, Kermit, 50, 53, 62

Roosevelt, Quentin, 48, 50–53, 62, 83

Roosevelt, Theodore "Teddy," 11, 20–21, 25, 45, 48, 50–52, 57, 62, 72, 77, 80–84

Roosevelt, Theodore, Jr., 50, 62, 77

Rose Garden, 78

Rose Room, 54

Rucker, Joanna, 83

Saturday Night Live, 36

School, 60–62

Secret Service, 28, 32, 36, 48, 60, 68, 72–76, 82

Solarium, 60

South Lawn, 39, 47, 66–67

Taft, Charlie, 34–35, 46, 48, 52, 54, 66–67, 82

Taft, Helen, 66

Taft, Julia, 41, 44–45

Taft, Robert, 66

Taft, William, 34, 66

Taylor, Zachary, 77

Temple, Shirley, 24

Traveling, 82

Treaty Room, 62

Truman, Harry, 59

Truman, Margaret, 54

Tyler, Alice, 14

Tyler, Elizabeth, 14

Tyler, John, 14, 80

Tyler, Letitia, 14

Tyler, Tazewell, 14

U.S. Capitol, 10, 46

Van Buren, Martin, 44, 52

Velocipede, 65

Washington, DC, 4, 8–9, 10

Washington, George, 8, 60, 77

Washington, Martha, 6, 8, 15, 60

Watusi, 28–29

Weddings, 21, 78–79

Whitman, Walt, 80

White House, the, 7, 11

Wilson, Woodrow, 48

World War II, 24, 47

Wright Brothers flying machine, 66–67

Yellow Drawing Room, 62

PHOTO CREDITS

. . . .